THE U SOLUTION

COLLEGE SUCCESS FROM CLASSROOM TO DORM ROOM AND EVERYWHERE IN-BETWEEN

JOSHUA D. SHEFFER

The U Solution
Copyright © 2016 Joshua D. Sheffer
All rights reserved.

ISBN: 978-1-943526-65-9 (paperback)
ISBN: 978-1-943526-64-2 (hard cover)

Library of Congress Control Number: 2016911232
Author Academy Elite, Powell, OH

CONTENTS

To my amazing wife Tara, for encouraging me to follow my dreams, and putting up with me while I did.

FOREWORD

COLLEGE—not only is it a completely new experience, but it also marks a major life transition. When an experience is this paramount and this life changing, is there ever a way to be totally ready for it?

Can students actually prepare for the academic rigors, the social mazes, and the potential dangers of college life?

Author Joshua D. Sheffer has always had a desire to help college students be successful. He enjoys teaching and helping students so much that, at one point, he taught a full load of courses at a local college while part of a nationwide law practice representing victims and survivors of school violence. He has now accepted his first appointment in full-time academia where he teaches legal studies to university undergraduates.

Joshua also founded U Ready, LLC, where the "U" stands for both "you" and "university." Joshua knows that complete success and fulfillment means different things to different people, and that college success is not a one-size-fits-all solution.

Unlike many other college preparation books, *The U Solution* does not focus solely on academic success or "college hacks." Instead it centers on providing information, tools, and strategies necessary for total college success.

But what really sets *The U Solution* apart from other college guides is Joshua's experience both as a professor and a lawyer. As a professor Joshua has seen what most students need help with; and as a lawyer, he has seen some of the most disastrous consequences of hazing, sexual violence, and other campus issues that most students simply aren't ready for.

In *The U Solution*, Joshua equips students with tools and strategies they can use to avoid and overcome college pitfalls academically, socially, mentally, and emotionally.

As Joshua likes to ask, "U Ready?" Maybe not right this second, but *The U Solution* will help you get there—safe, sound, and successful.

Kary Oberbrunner

CEO of Igniting Souls. Co-creator of Author Academy Elite. Author of *Elixir Project, Day Job to Dream Job, The Deeper Path,* and *Your Secret Name.*

ORIENTATION
WHY?

So, you bought this book (or someone bought it for you) hoping it will help you succeed at college. Why this book?

Why any book?

Shouldn't you just go off to college and wing it?

These are all questions you may be asking. And if you are asking these questions, great! Questioning the things you encounter, testing them for their value, and making your own decisions about whether something is beneficial will help you be successful in college and the rest of your life.

There are answers to these questions, and to many others you may have. To answer the last question first—No. You should not just go off to college and wing it. Why go into a situation unprepared? Preparation invites success and college is such a pivotal time in life. Position yourself for success. It can't hurt, right?

This book will prepare you for the challenges posed by college. The ones you already know about, and the ones you will learn about as you read. You'll receive tools and strategies for overcoming the obstacles that often enter the paths of even the best high school students and most well-intentioned students starting college.

I want your college experience to be enjoyable and successful. I don't want college to be something you "get through." You should enjoy your experience and flourish in every way. I hope this book plays some role in helping you reach that success.

Why listen to me?

Several things in my life led me to write this book. I've been where you are, and I know that having some of these tools in my toolbox would have made my college life a little easier. But I've also seen a lot from many different angles after I graduated from college and law school.

As a professor, I've seen that many students lack some core tools that could help them increase their success. For instance, I've seen both good and poor students struggle with time management—but, more often than not, good students have at least passable time management skills. And even students that did all right would have been more successful, and had more free time, if they had possessed certain time-management tools. Many topics covered in this book were chosen for similar reasons.

Other topics included are based on my experience seeing younger friends go through school—some successfully, some not—and from things I saw while I practiced law. These are topics like the need to improve written communication and learning to find resources when you need help.

Some topics in this book, especially those covered in Part III, stemmed from my experience as part of a nationwide law practice representing survivors, victims, and—in the worst instances—families of victims of school violence. While practicing in this area of law, I looked deeply into the worlds of hazing, sexual assault, bullying, and even school shootings. These problems need to be eradicated, and I want to help you both avoid them, and be part of the solution.

What this book isn't, and what it is.

This book is a tool to help you prepare for and succeed during college. It's not a list of tips, tricks, and hacks to help you choose the correct multiple-choice test answer or solve each specific disagreement with your roommate. I won't be teaching you how to solve that function in your Calculus 203 course or giving you the outline to use on your English 107 paper. There are books out there like that, but this is not one.

Another thing this book is not: a survival guide. A survival guide teaches you how to make it—this book is a success guide; it can help you *own* it. This is a guide to thrive, not merely survive.

I've divided the book into three parts: Gen. Ed.—Prerequisites; B.A.—Basic Academics; and B.S.—Being Successful. Many concepts will overlap. The first section, *Gen. Ed.,* lays a foundation for the rest of the book, and for a certain outlook on both college and life. This section deals with defining success and some of the most important tools to take with you throughout your entire college experience and into life after school.

The second section, *B.A.—Basic Academics,* covers certain areas and ideas that will help you achieve your academic potential; things like time management, improving your writing, study strategies, and more. These aren't "school hacks" or "tricks," but tools and skills to put you on the right path and in the right frame of mind.

Finally, *B.S.—Being Successful,* covers many things you may not have even known you needed to think about—from forming your social circle to the dangers of hazing and sexual assault. This section will point out some real problems that many college students face, but it will also demonstrate how to avoid falling prey to these dangers. And more importantly, you will encounter strategies and tools to help you be part of the solution to many of these problems that plague college campuses.

How to use this book.

This is not the type of book that is best used by waiting for a problem to crop up and then looking up the solution. This book is much better used as a preemptive tool to avoid common problems students face. Don't wait until you're cramming the night before your calculus exam to pull out this book and read the chapters on study strategies and time management. They won't help you ace that test (but they will help you do better on the next one).

Read this book before you start school, before you move into the dorms. Read it as soon as you can after you've decided that going away to college is your next step. This will give you time to incorporate the strategies into your life.

This book gives you tools and resources to succeed. It's a starting point. It won't give you all the answers, and it's not supposed to. It's kind of like a long-form movie trailer: I'll show you the plot, the challenge, and some glimpses of the action, but you'll have to invest more time if you want the entire, inside scoop.

And, because who doesn't like multiple metaphors, this book will help you lay the foundation for building college success. It's not the entire building, but it will give you a strong base to add to.

Make no mistake: there is no magic pill (or book) that will guarantee your college success, but there are tools available to help everyone succeed. This book is one of those tools, and is the first step toward your success. Other resources are also available, and you should definitely use them.

College success isn't for the special few who were born with "what it takes." It is not reserved for those who were straight-A high school students—it's not even guaranteed for them. College success is only reserved for the lucky. If you want to be one of the "lucky ones" who have great college success, remember:

An old Irish Proverb states, "There is no luck except where there is discipline."

Ben Franklin said, "Diligence is the mother of good luck."

And the Roman philosopher Seneca famously said, "Luck is what happens when preparation meets opportunity."

Everyone will tell you what a great opportunity college is. Let's work on the preparation part.

GEN. ED.—
PREREQUISITES

GEOGRAPHY
WHERE AM I AND WHAT AM I DOING HERE?

High school is different for everyone. Some people love it and think of it as the time of their lives; others struggle socially, academically, or both. Some go to big schools, others to extremely small high schools. But if you're ready in this book, you all have many things in common, too. One thing is that you've either graduated or are well on your way to graduating, and you're preparing yourself for college.

And there are other similarities. Almost all of you will have also had a regular schedule. You'd start in August or September and, but for a few relatively short vacations, you went to school every weekday from 8 am to 3 pm (or something like that) until May or June. You may not have had the same classes every day, but you were there for the same amount of time.

After school, you went home to your family and, likely, had a relatively regular routine; maybe it included extracurricular activities, a job, or something else. And no matter how responsible you were for your own activities, or being where you had to be when you were supposed to be there, you probably had a support system that at least provided you with reminders or a little assistance toward getting where you needed to be and finishing all of the things you needed to get done. Not to mention that no matter how free you were to do whatever you wanted on weekends, your parents probably wanted to know what you were up to. Even the most self-reliant, freedom-enjoying high school student has had some tethers he or she didn't even realize were there. And these are good things, things you may have taken for granted, or even complained about or rebelled against. But these things were there, and they helped.

Then there's college. Get ready for life to completely change, especially if you go away to school. Things are about to get really, really different. You may think you know exactly what's going to be different and that you are ready for whatever comes your way, but can anyone truly be ready for such a sea change in so many aspects of life all at once?

Where am I?

Whoa.

College.

You made it; you graduated from high school.

You're here, about to start college.

But what does it all mean?

There are many different ways of looking at college. And people aren't usually too shy about telling you what they think your view of college should be.

As a professor, I've seen many students who simply view college as high school 2.0. This can be especially prevalent if you go away to college with a bunch of people who graduated high school with you. A "high school 2.0" view of college sees college as 13th grade. Those with this view don't look at college as a big step or major change; they only see it as what you do after you graduate from high school. Not always, but often, this causes a student to fail to take college seriously. If you're there for no other reason than "it's what you do," why care any more than you did in high school?

While some students took high school very seriously—you probably know a couple of people of whom you'd say took it *too seriously*—and got away with the high school 2.0 approach, this isn't always the case. Students who take the high school 2.0 view usually struggle when they start to take classes where the academic expectations are significantly higher than in their high school classes, or when they realize that the note-taking and study strategies they used in high school may not work in college.

I've also heard people describe college as "career training." This view of college is tempting. If you've always known exactly what you want to do, then it's easy to look at college merely as the training you need to get there. And for parents who want to see college lead directly to financial success for their children, or for whoever is footing the astronomical bill of most colleges, a "career training" view helps them see college as an investment that will pay off down the line.

Concentrating on the "career training" view of college can lead to academic success, if the student is truly motivated in that regard, but it can have negative consequences, too. For one, this view leaves out some significant aspects of college, like social development and self-discovery. And it fails to recognize the reality that many people happily—and successfully—spend their lives after college in a career entirely different from what they studied in school.

Research and data compiled by members of the Federal Reserve Bank of New York's Research and Statistics Group found that only about 27% of undergraduate degree holders are working in a job directly related to their college major.[1]

I fit into this category of people whose career does not match their undergraduate degree—to an extent anyway. I started out thinking of college as career training, and declared a double major in physics and engineering. My plan was to become an electrical engineer. I changed my major more than once and graduated (on time) with a bachelor of arts in philosophy and a minor in Japanese. Had I entered the "real world" from there, my career options would have been limited. So I went to graduate school. I ended up in law school, graduated, and practiced law for 15 years before realizing that I wasn't following my dreams or being true to who I was, and now I'm beginning my second career in my dream job as a university professor.

Much of this is to say that the real drawback to looking at college from a pure "career training" view assumes that sometime between the ages of 18-24 you're going to know exactly what you want to do as a career for the rest of your life. That's a bunch of pressure—a whole bunch of pressure.

Still others treat college as a place for pure self-discovery and for learning life lessons. Many of these people have the mistaken view that "what happens in college stays in college." While this view of college certainly has some strong points—we all need to discover who we are, what we dream of, and what we want to be and achieve—it can also lead to ignoring the fact that actions have consequences. Not too different from this are the people who have already decided that college is going to be "the best time of my life." Now, I certainly think that everyone going to college should think that it is going to be the best part of their life *up to that point*. But please, *please* don't convince yourself that it's all going to be downhill after college. If done right, post-college life is great, and you should always know that the best is yet to come.

So, what's the right answer? Which is the best way to look at college? Is it just the next logical step after your graduation, high school 2.0? Is it a huge step, a really big deal? When you start college, are you training for your future career, or are you just learning to be yourself?

Is it all of these things?

None of them?

Ultimately, you're the only one who can answer the question. How you view college does matter, but it is not the be-all-end-all of success. Many people who view college as simply the thing you do after high school fail to take it seriously enough, but others do. Some people who view college as the biggest deal ever and look at every grade as having a direct bearing on their entire future stress themselves beyond the ability to succeed, but others do just fine.

So how you look at college matters. I'm not going to tell you what the "right" view is because I don't think there is one. Any extreme is likely a "wrong" view. The important thing is that you are honest with yourself about what you are doing at college, and that you look at it in a way that gets you to take it seriously, but keep it in perspective.

What am I doing here?

And if there are so many different ways to view what college even is, what does college success look like?

Is success getting good grades?

Is it finding out who you are and what you love?

Is it making the right connections to get the right career and earn a lot of money?

Some combination?

Something else entirely?

7

Again, the most important part is that you are honest with yourself about what you are trying to achieve in college. But make this decision wisely. Hold your beliefs securely but openly. Have real reasons for your choice, but be willing to change with new information. Don't just assume that you know why you're there and that the reason will never change. Trust me, you don't have to make a decision on how you're going to define success at college before you start, and then stick with it come what may. I'm not going to leave a blank here for you to write down your chosen view of college and your parameters for success, and then ask you to sign your name, making an unchangeable declaration for all time. That would be ridiculous.

Success will invariably mean different things to different people. It may mean something different to your friends than it does to you. It may mean something else entirely to your parents. It may mean one thing to you now, and something different after a semester or two at college. But it is important that you think about what success means to you, and that you measure yourself against *your* goals. Don't ignore others' definitions of success, but don't accept them without question either. Take them all into account and use them to help discover what success means to you.

If you measure yourself solely against others' goals for you, then you will never feel successful, no matter how well you meet those goals. You need to succeed for you, in the way that matters to you.

Yes, you need to study hard and get good grades. Flunking out of college is never part of a successful college experience. Success doesn't have to mean graduating at the top of your class (but it could).

When you think about success as purely academic achievement, or when you start to stress about a less-than-stellar grade, remember this: What do you call the person who graduates last in class from medical school?

Doctor.

The person who finishes last ends up with the same title as the person who finishes first. Now, the person finishing last may not have the same pick of jobs after medical school, but he or she is still a doctor. And finishing at the top of the class in college doesn't necessarily make you better at your career than someone who finished with lower grades. There's so much more to it; grades may be important, but they're not life or death.

Whether your definition of success includes getting top grades, building your self-confidence, or anything else, there is one overarching piece that must be in everyone's success definition: becoming the best you. This may sound trite or cliché, but it' also true. Self-exploration, networking, career training—whatever your definition of success is, it must include self-growth.

Total college success is a combination of academic achievement, social experience, and generally equipping you to take on the challenges that await you after college is finished. Learning who you are and what your passions are, growing and maturing into the type of person you want to be— these are as, or more, important than getting straight A's.

But hey, there's no reason you can't do all of that other stuff *and* get great grades.

And I don't mean there's no reason *people* can do all of these things and get great grades. I mean *you* can. With a realistic and holistic definition of success, you can achieve all you want in college. You are capable of getting the same or better grades than you got in high school, you are capable of learning to speak in public and write masterfully. You are able to ace that math, history, science, or [insert scariest subject for you here] class.

Start here, with this book. Get the basics. Find out what you still need, then get that, either through our U Ready programs or elsewhere. Success is not an unattainable goal; it's there for you to grab it.

You got this.

ECONOMICS
NOTHING IS FREE

T his chapter has nothing to do with how much money it costs to go to school.
Not.
A.
Thing.
In fact, it's not about money at all. This is about a larger principle, something that affects students paying their own way at the most expensive private school available and those with full scholarships and living stipends all the same.

When I tell you here that nothing is free, I'm saying that every decision, every choice, even every goal, has a trade-off. Nothing is free. Choices have consequences; some good, some bad, and some neutral. Whether some consequences are good or bad will depend on your goals, and something may be a good consequence today and not-so-good in a couple of weeks. The important thing to know is that everything has some kind of cost.

Your decisions must be *your* decisions. But you should know that they are decisions that, like all other decisions, have some ramifications. Sure, there are many decisions that are more inconsequential than others, like which foods to grab at the dining hall for lunch or whether to wear a sweatshirt today. And not all decisions require a long, drawn out weighing of pros, cons, and possible future consequences. The key is to be aware that decisions are always a choice among options available.

And even if there doesn't seem to be a cost to your decision, there is always at least the cost of not making the other decision available at the time. Again, these are not life-or-death choices all the time, or even most of the time.

We are our choices.

- Jean-Paul Sartre

One's philosophy is not best expressed in words; it is expressed in the choices one makes... and the choices we make are ultimately our responsibility.

- Eleanor Roosevelt

These quotes are a couple different ways of saying, "Actions speak louder than words." You've heard that phrase many times throughout your life; heck, you've probably said it more than a few times. And it's completely true.

We can say all sorts of things about ourselves, about what we believe, about how we think, and if we don't back it up with the way we act, we don't really believe it. I'm sure you're familiar with public figures who spend most of their lives projecting a wholesome, family-friendly version of themselves only to have their choices, actions they chose to commit, come to light and completely change everyone's perception of them.

If I were to ask you which version was true—the carefully cultivated public image that lasted for years or the corrupted, not-so-wholesome version presented by the person's actions that finally came to light—you'd undoubtedly tell me it was the person revealed by the actions. Because you can say all the right things about yourself, and others can say all the right things about you, but your actions tell a lot about you.

Take, for instance, Sir Robin from Monty Python's Holy Grail—please tell me you've seen the movie; it's still a thing, right? Just in case you haven't seen it, it's a classic British comedy about King Arthur and the Knights of the Round Table seeking the Holy Grail and going on various adventures. One of the knights in the film is Sir Robin. Sir Robin is constantly followed by bards singing of his never-ending bravery.

In one scene, Robin and his bards are alone when they come across a three-headed knight. The three heads of the three-headed knight begin arguing. When the three-headed knight finally decides to kill Sir Robin, the heads look down to find that Sir Robin has fled. The film then cuts to Sir Robin and his bards, who are now singing:

> *Brave Sir Robin ran away, bravely ran away, away;*
> *When danger reared its ugly head, he bravely turned*
> *his tail and fled.* [2]

And the verse continues with wonderful lines about how Sir Robin "gallantly… chickened out" and "beat a very brave retreat."

Sir Robin's reputation was for bravery, but his choices were not brave. And even though the bards are still singing that Sir Robin is so brave, when they describe the actions he chose, it is clear that he is not. Sir Robin said he was brave. The bards said Sir Robin was brave. Then Sir Robin made a very not-brave choice, letting everyone know that, no matter how often he and everyone else had said otherwise, he *was not* brave.

At least in that moment he wasn't. Maybe he was almost always brave; maybe even every time but in that one instance. But since that's the only moment we ever see when he has a chance to be brave, and he's not, we judge him on the choice he made right then.

Everyone makes mistakes. No doubt there will be points in your life when you go against what you really believe for one reason or another. But actions do speak louder than words. And when you do go against the things you say you are, the people who see you do it are going to doubt you until you prove them otherwise. It's so much harder to undo a reputation based on your actions than one based on your words.

> *It's our choices, Harry, that show what we truly are, far more than our abilities.*
>
> - **Professor Dumbledore, in *Harry Potter and the Chamber of Secrets* by J.K. Rowling**

If the first quotes were about actions being louder than words, this quote is about your choices being louder than your natural, or even honed, abilities. Natural talent and abilities can only take you so far, and the wrong choices can even take away or negate your natural abilities.

I'm sure you've heard someone describe another person as a natural at something. "She's got a gift," or "He doesn't even practice." Natural talent is a great start to a lot of things, but it seldom takes someone all the way. If you're a sports fan, you've heard or seen about the soon-to-be-pro athlete who has so much "upside" or "potential." And you've also seen how many of those people never realize their full potential and become the great players all the analysts thought they had a chance to be.

It's the same with school. There are a lot of people with the natural abilities to float through high school without working too hard at it. Sometimes these people can get pretty far in college, too. But they won't be able to get by on their natural talent forever. Sooner or later, they will need to hone it, to develop it, or it will just go to waste.

You have to choose to make yourself better. Choose to do the right thing. Choose to take whatever natural gifts, talents, and abilities you've been given and shape them into your vision of success. If you want to get good grades at college, you can. It may not be easy, but you can do it. You'll be introduced to a lot of helpful tools throughout this book, but you have to choose to use them. If you choose to use the tools and resources available, you may have to work hard, but you can be a successful college student.

And trust me, professors can usually tell who is working hard and who isn't. We can tell who enjoys the class or really wants to learn from the people who are just there because it's a requirement. And teaching someone who is only there because they have to be just isn't that much fun or rewarding. Especially when, even if it's a class that you wouldn't take unless you had to, you can still choose to learn the material and try to get something out of the course.

Sure, it's nice to teach people who have a natural gift toward learning and understanding the subject matter. But it's much more rewarding and fun to teach someone who chooses to try to learn, chooses to be interested in the subject, and chooses to actually care about things.

JOSHUA D. SHEFFER

*How we spend our days is, of course,
how we spend our lives.*

- **Annie Dillard**

This is probably my favorite quote about choices, even though it never uses the word. If actions speak louder than words, and our choices make us who we are more than our abilities do, then the choices we make ultimately define who we are and how we lead our lives. Each little choice may not matter so much on its own, but over time our choices add up.

If you choose to stay by yourself and study constantly, never making time for anyone or anything else, it will ultimately affect who you are. If you choose to view everything negative in your life as punishment or a sign from the universe that no one really likes you, it will change who you are.

And if you choose to always put yourself first, and "look out for number one" come what may, you will spend your life as a selfish person. When you look back on your life, you probably won't remember every choice that led you to becoming the person you are, but you likely remember a few of them. And if you want to change who you are, you need to start changing the choices you make. You can't just look at the big goal and say, "This is how I want to live and how I want people to see me and remember me," and then make choices that go against that goal. The little choices lead us on the path.

The things we do on a day-to-day basis add up. And once you've created a pattern for the choices you make, and who you are, it can sometimes be hard to change them. I don't know that this is what Annie Dillard meant when she wrote the quote, but that's what I get from it. It's the little things, the small moments, the choices we make about what to do right now that, when we look back, make up our life.

Dillard uses the saying as a springboard to talk about schedules and looking at life instead of individual days, which is also very powerful. She talks about a schedule defending from chaos, mocking up reason and order; making each day the same. Because you likely won't remember individual days, but you will be able to look back on your life later and see a powerful pattern.[3]

Think about what you think of as a good life. Often, what we think about as a good life doesn't necessarily make up a good day. Dillard talks specifically of a day spent reading versus a life spent reading. A day full of reading might not seem like a good day to a lot of people, although some may think it the best day ever, but a life spent reading, spent learning and growing, is a good life. But you cannot achieve the life of reading if you never choose the days of reading.

If you have a goal, start working toward it. Don't wait to start tomorrow, or next week, or next year, or after college, or after *anything*. If there is something you want, start working on it now. Start making the choices each day that will lead you to that life.

Switching metaphors

I almost called this chapter "Physics—Actions and Reactions," because that is another part of choices and how everything you do matters in one way or another. And because physics can be fun. I would know; I spent a *whole semester* at college majoring in physics. For what it's worth, I ended up majoring in Philosophy, which was a lot of fun, and minoring in Japanese, also fun.

But I didn't go straight with a physics theme for this chapter because while it is important to know that your actions cause reactions and your choices cause effects, it's also important to think of your choices as having, at the very least, an opportunity cost.

"Opportunity cost" is an economic concept that means even if something doesn't have a tangible cost of money or goods, everything you do costs you the opportunity of doing something else at the same time. This is a classic trope found in both movies and television, where someone wishes they could be in two places at once. It leads to the episode where the character is trying to juggle two dates at the same time; or sometimes, there is a clone or a doppelganger meant to handle one of the tasks, usually the less desirable one, while the original does something else. And *it never ends well*. When you try to get around the opportunity cost, it ends up costing so much more. In virtually every movie or television show where a character tries to avoid the opportunity cost by taking both opportunities, he or she ends up messing up their opportunities and coming away with neither. Unless it's a romantic comedy, then the character 'fesses up, a love song plays, everyone immediately laughs about the ill-conceived hijinks, and they all live happily ever after. *This almost never happens in real life.*

Every party you go to, or every moment you spend watching TV in your room, is time you *do not* spend doing something else. Same with every moment you spend studying. You can only do one thing at a time. And there's nothing wrong with looking at the opportunity cost when you make your decisions. But you should look at the immediate opportunity cost and the opportunity cost down the road; if you decide to go hang out with your friends this weekend and blow off your paper that's not due for a couple weeks, that may be fine, but you won't be able to blow it off next weekend too. So, if you know there's something you want to do next weekend, that's part of the opportunity cost of not working on your paper this weekend.

But now that we've talked some about choices and dealt with opportunity cost, let's switch classes, and do some physics.

Actions and Reactions

Some of Isaac Newton's famous physics contributions are the three Newtonian Laws of Motion. The third law of motion is, "For every action, there is an equal and opposite reaction." And although Newton meant this when talking about forces acting on objects, it applies more than passably to many other real-life situations.

Okay, now it's time for another earth-shattering truth you really need to know: Professors are people, too. I know, it's hard to believe, but it's true. And, as people, professors have the same range or emotions, responses, highs, and lows as any other person does, even students.

Crazy, right?

Every moment your professors spend teaching you, grading your exams and papers, meeting with you outside of class, preparing class materials, arranging for you to take a late exam, working with the school's computer system to enter a grade on that overdue assignment you just turned in—each and every one of those moments—is one they could be spending doing something else. And although most professors chose their profession for a reason, and don't mind too much doing the regular things that come with the job, and a significant amount of extra time in many cases, they have things they'd rather be doing.

Trust me on this: for every moment you spend taking that essay exam, wishing you could be doing something else, your professor has those moments, multiplied by the students who took the exam, as he or she grades the exams. It's really not fun.

But when students put in the work and try to learn the material and really get something out of it, professors notice. And when a student is trying, professors are less grumpy about spending some extra time helping that student. If you turn in almost all of your assignments on time, and they show effort, your professor will probably be a little more lenient about that one you need to turn in late. If you're a good student who comes to exams prepared, your professor will probably go a little further to let you reschedule the exam because you have a scheduling conflict.[1]

It's not just in interactions with professors, though. There are also equal and opposite reactions to other choices and decisions you make. If you choose to go to that party (or *those parties*) the weekend before your big exam instead of studying, it will likely affect your performance on the exam. If your professor gives you eight weeks to write a paper that makes up a huge percentage of your grade, and you wait until the last couple of days to do it, it'll likely affect your grade. These are actions that have reactions.

But the reactions don't only flow that way. Study constantly and never leave your room to hang out with friends? They'll eventually stop asking, and you'll likely build up so much stress over your grades that you can't think about anything else. Sleep in every day and skip breakfast to avoid being late for class? Your doctor will tell you there are effects from that, too.

---

[1]   Some professors, though, have been burned so many times that they have very strict policies that they adhere to in all cases. These are usually spelled out in the course syllabus you'll get in one of the first class sessions or will be available online. If your professor has written policies on late work or makeup exams, be sure to know what they are.

Inertia

Newton's first law of motion can be summarized as "Objects in motion tend to stay in motion; objects at rest tend to stay at rest unless an outside force acts upon them." In essence, that chair in your room isn't going to move unless somebody moves it, but (except for friction) that ball that you throw isn't going to stop unless someone stops it.

This can apply to you too, much in the same way as "How you live your days is how you live your life." This will go into so much of what you do. If you study a little bit each day, you'll get in the habit of studying, and it will get easier for you to make the time. If you party all the time, it will be super hard to change it up, buckle down and study for that exam or get that paper done on time.

There is something to be said for inertia, routine, and momentum. You want to avoid a rut, but not all habits and routines are ruts. You're in a rut when you keep doing the same things and going nowhere. Routines that help you achieve your goals can be helpful and exciting. And even if they don't seem exciting in the moment, you'll be able to look back and see your progress after even a little time.

Just make sure your inertia keeps pushing you toward your goals. Don't stay in one place—that's not why you decided to go to college in the first place. You're looking to get somewhere, to make a difference, to do something with your life. So do it. Get yourself there.

Public Speaking
Confidence is Key

Picture this: Mid-August, 8:00 on a Monday morning, about 60 students starting their very first class of their very first year of law school; the professor, a well-respected and imposing lawyer, gets up and says, "Everyone look to your right. Now look to your left. One of the three of you will not be at this school by the end of the school year."

Encouraging, right? Thankfully, that's not the way I started law school (my first class started at 9:00). But I've heard stories of more than one professor who started classes that way. Apparently, professors who do this think that a little "healthy fear" causes their students to buckle down and work harder to prove that they're one of the two that will remain.

I had a professor later that day who started class a little differently. Once everyone sat down and he took attendance, he said something like this, "If you're here, and you're sitting there thinking that somehow you slipped through the cracks; that you're not smart enough to be here; not as good as everyone else; if that's you, look around the room. Everyone else is feeling the same thing. You belong here.

You're smart enough; you didn't slip through the cracks. You belong here."

I'm sure there were some people "inspired" by the first professor's words—if by inspired you mean scared out of their wits and overstressed to the point where they're convinced they need to study and work 24/7 to prove that they're not going to be the one in three that doesn't make it. But I know for sure that the second example was what I needed to hear, and I think it is what more students need to hear. Most people don't accidentally fall into college. And certainly, with as many applicants as there are to most schools, colleges have refined their selection practices to the point where people don't ordinarily slip through the cracks and sneak into a college environment where they don't belong academically. If you made it into college, you have what it takes to make it out of college successfully.

So, when you first sit down in a class where you feel like you don't belong, where you feel like you're not smart enough to be there: look to your left and look to your right; both those people are probably feeling the same thing.

One of the worst things you can do to yourself is accept, or even create, undue stress. Trust me, there will always be enough normal stress available that you don't need to create or bring your own.

How to be confident.

It's one thing to know you can be more successful if you're confident; it's something entirely different to actually *be* confident. Similarly, knowing you should be confident is different from believing it and even more different than actually *being* confident.

Confidence is not false bravado or cockiness; those *never* come across well. And if you try to fake confidence, that is what it will come off as. A strong, quiet confidence is powerful. And that is precisely the confidence you need.

So how do you get there?

There are several different paths to confidence, and like the other things we talk about in Part 1—Prerequisites, you must find your own. There are some common paths, and some universal steps, but you must ultimately find the way that works for you.

One universal step toward true confidence is preparation. This book and other U Ready resources will certainly help you there. You can be confident when you know what to expect and you have a plan, or at least an idea, of how you will deal with it.

Confidence requires knowing and accepting who you are. If you don't know yourself, how can you be confident in yourself? This is probably the hardest step toward confidence. Learning who you are is not necessarily easy, but things worth doing rarely are. Sometimes, the hardest part about learning who you are is accepting the good things about yourself.

I guarantee you're good at something. I'll take that further: I guarantee you're good at many things.

What are they?

Do you accept that you're good at these things, or do you downplay it or say something self-deprecating when someone compliments you?

A secret about life that takes many people way too long to learn: *when someone compliments you, it's okay to say, "Thank you."* You don't have to pretend it's no big deal, or that you're no more talented/haven't worked harder than anyone else. If you're being complimented on something that you worked hard to achieve, it's perfectly fine to say something along the lines of, "Thanks, I've been practicing for a long time," or, "Thank you, I've worked really hard to learn to do that."

As long as you're authentic about it, that's a perfectly good way to accept a compliment. And you know what?

You deserve it.

If you really did work hard to master a skill or develop a talent, own it. You've earned that.

And if you constantly downplay your efforts, other people may actually think you're bragging. They may think you believe yourself such a natural talent that you were able to pick up that skill without any effort.

Or maybe they'll take you at your word and believe that it's nothing special. And I guess that's all well and good, but eventually, you may even convince yourself that you aren't anything special; that you can't do anything that can't be done by everyone else. Here's what you need to remember:

That's

Not

True.

Not everyone can do what you do. Sure, there may be some people in the world that are better at certain things than you are, even the things you're good at. But you're you.

Accept you.

It may sound trite, but love you.

Knowing you and accepting you are the first steps toward confidence.

One step at a time.

There's a prayer that's been around for nearly 100 years, if not longer. No matter where you stand on faith, this prayer has some real truths. So much so that it's been adopted by many 12-step programs. You've probably heard some version of this:

Grant me the serenity to accept the things I cannot change;
The courage to change the things I can;
And the wisdom to know the difference.

Why do I bring this up?

Because an honest assessment of your life and your circumstances through this lens can really build true confidence. Let's look at how:

The things I cannot change.

There are certain things in life that are, indeed, beyond your control. Some completely beyond your control, like the weather or the due date for that big physics assignment. There are other things that are *mostly* out of your control but that you can still influence or have a say in. This includes things like who wins an election or how your school deals with an important issue.

With the things completely beyond your control, you have to let go. Stop thinking you can control them and stop trying to control them. The more you try to control things that you have no ability to even effectively influence, the more you will stress yourself out. And the more you stress yourself out, the more anxious you become, the more you imagine the worst, and the less likely you are to achieve your best.

With the things you have some influence over, but are mostly out of your control, you do your best to reach your desired outcome, but you must ultimately let go and accept the results even if they don't go your way. Know the level of influence you really had, and don't beat yourself up or stress out if it just doesn't go your way.

Many people are closet control freaks—wanting to be in charge of everything and to control how everything plays out and ends up. But no one can control it all. You can influence other people, but you can't force them to change. You can make sure you recycle everything possible, but you can't ensure that landfills don't grow. You know, you can lead a horse to water, but you can't make it drink.

One thing you really need to know you can't change is the past. You can do things to make past situations have less of an effect on the future, but you can't make them go away like they never happened. So, if you did something embarrassing or made a mistake in the past, do your best to remedy it, but there's no use beating yourself up about it. *You can't make it unhappen.* If you did make a mistake: accept it, grow from it, and if it harmed someone or something, try to make it right. But don't take on unending guilt. Don't let it define you. Do what you can to fix any damage you caused, and then let go.

On a similar note, it does no good to pretend that the past didn't happen, or to try to cover it up, and to live in fear that you will be discovered and then something bad will happen. If you made a mistake, don't try to hide it.

Own it.

Own up to it.

Remedy any damage you can.

Learn and grow from it.

And move on.

So when it comes to the things you cannot change, you must accept them and let go. This is not to say that you have to like them, but it does no good for you to cause yourself undue stress about something that *you didn't cause or you can't change.*

And this will help your confidence.

How?

If you accept that you cannot change certain things, then you'll no longer doubt yourself and you won't beat yourself up when things you can't control don't go your way.

If you don't hold yourself accountable for things you can't change, then you can't lower your confidence when they don't go your way—it's not on you.

Accept the things you cannot change.

Refuse to own what doesn't belong to you.

The things I can change

There's a lot you can change.

Most importantly for confidence, you need to understand that you can change an awful lot about yourself. Sure, without fancy (and probably expensive) medical procedures, you can't change things like your height or other physical characteristics. But when it comes to your immediate circumstances and how you respond to them, you have control. Don't believe the excuses.

If you're too tired all of the time and having a hard time staying awake in class or following the lecture, then go to bed earlier, eat healthier, take naps, exercise, or use one of several other _healthy_ techniques to help you stay awake and focus. This, you can change.

Don't like the grade you got on that paper? Don't believe it when you try to tell yourself "you're just not a good writer." That's not true. While some people may be gifted, natural writers, anyone can learn to write more-than-passably well. This, you can change.

Having a hard time understanding that concept you're about to be tested on? It's not that "you're just not good at math," or that "you just aren't smart enough to get it." Take advantage of resources available for tutoring or extra instruction. This, you can change.

When you are honest with yourself about the things you can change, even the difficult things, you can start to make changes. And when you start changing things you have power to change, making your life and circumstances better, you can't help but be more confident.

Knowing you are in control of things is empowering, especially after you've let go of the things you know you can't control. Even more empowering: *exercising that control to better yourself.*

Once you start exercising the control you have and changing things for the better, your confidence will naturally rise.

Knowing the difference.

The "wisdom to know the difference" is key—you must be honest about which things you can change and which you can't. It can be easy to start classifying things as beyond your control. And the harder it is for you to control or influence something, the easier it is to convince yourself that it's something you cannot change.

Can you control the outcome of a presidential election?

No, but it certainly doesn't mean you shouldn't exercise your right to vote.

And once you've exercised your right to vote, it would be wrong to then sit back and say, "It's out of my control. I can't do anything else about it now." Because that is not true; you can campaign, educate, and rally.

You're not being honest with yourself if you say that something is a situation you cannot change unless you do everything within your power to make a difference. And if you're not honest with yourself on this issue, you will erode your own confidence by asking yourself what more you could have done. "If I had x, would y have happened?" or "Why didn't I try a?" If you have done everything in your power, truly done your best, you don't have to ask yourself these questions.

Applying the "things I cannot change" label to something you do have control over also directly disempowers you. If you reduce your own agency, your own ability to affect outcomes, then you are taking power away from yourself. By saying, "I cannot change x" when you can, you are telling yourself you are weaker than you are. This is detrimental to confidence.

So, look at your circumstances. If there's something you don't like, look at it through the lens of accepting what you can't change, changing what you can, and knowing the difference. The more honest you are with yourself, the more confident you can be in the world around you.

Preparation

Another key part of confidence is preparation; and a key part of preparation is awareness. But awareness, without more, is worthless. Awareness without strategy can actually cause more stress. Anticipation without a plan can cause serious anxiety. That's why this book is more than just telling you what you'll face—it also provides you with foundational tools and strategies to help you overcome those things.

Once you're aware, you can prepare.

If you're prepared, you don't need to be anxious.

So if you want to be confident going into that big exam, study for it and be prepared. This isn't a "study all night right before the exam" preparation, though. If you want to be confident, you need to be really prepared. You need to start studying as soon as you begin learning the material. Commit it to memory while it's fresh. Then, as the exam nears, you'll be more confident to begin with.

Review sessions the night before the exam are great, *study* sessions aren't. But we'll cover that more in Part 2: B.A.—Basic Academics.

But it's not just being prepared for exams or papers that makes you more confident. You can prepare for anything. If you know you're going to have a conversation that could be difficult, make sure you know the message you are trying to get across and the reasons behind that message before you enter into the conversation. This won't guarantee the conversation will go smoothly, but at least you can be confident about your part in it. Just remember, preparation is different from running the conversation over and over in your head, with everything playing out the worst way possible every time. That doesn't help anyone.

It's all about you.

Confidence is all about you. But it's not self-centeredness, conceit, or egomania. Confidence comes from knowing yourself: knowing where you are, where you want to be, and having a plan to get there. If you know what is important to you, and you know what you can change and what you can't, then you can confidently approach and interact with the world around you.

So the world isn't all about you, but how you interact with it or let it affect you is. And knowing where your power lies, what you can or can't change, allows you a more realistic view of the world. And this realistic view allows you confidence. You don't have to be anxious about the things you can't change, because *it won't help*. You'll be able to focus your energy on the things you can change. Trust me, it'll be better.

What can I do about it?

There is a lot of great advice out there on how to be confident, or how to be more confident. But we'll end this chapter, which has been mostly "big picture," with a practical tip: start building confidence with something that's for you.

I'm sure there's something you've always been interested in learning. So today's tip to greater confidence: *learn it.* Learn it for no reason other than you're interested. Want to learn how to program computers? Find some books or online classes or other ways to learn to program. Want to learn how to juggle? I'm sure you can. Want to become an unofficial expert on bourgeois cuisine during the French Revolution? Go for it.

It can be something discrete, that you can learn and then you'll know how to do, or it can be the beginning of a life-long learning process. But if you find something you enjoy that you can learn, learning it will build your confidence. And if you're just learning it for you, then there will be nothing to be anxious about. And as you learn, you'll build confidence.

I got an extra boost in my confidence when I started studying kung fu. Learning something like a martial art and getting into better shape can be doubly beneficial to your confidence. First, you build confidence by learning a new thing. And you get a second boost because you feel less anxious in social situations because you know that you can take care of yourself, if necessary.

Although you should always have at least a little self-defense training before starting college, it is not necessary that you devote a large portion of your life to studying martial arts—that's just one example of something I've done that has been a huge confidence builder. Learning to play an instrument or teaching yourself about physics or photography or anything else will also help you build confidence.

B.A.—
BASIC ACADEMICS

LIFE SCIENCE
TIME MANAGEMENT

I t is nearly impossible to overstate the importance of time management and the impact that using appropriate time management strategies can have on your life. If you think that high school teachers occasionally assign too much homework, you'll likely learn to thank them for being easy on you. When I went to college, a couple more years ago than I'd like to say, it was said that for every hour of class, you should be ready for two hours of homework, on average. And that calculation did not include studying beyond your homework. Under those calculations, if you're taking 15 credit hours in a semester, you should be prepared for about 30 hours of homework each week. And if you want to be really academically successful, you should dedicate some extra time to purely studying on top of that.

That can make for a pretty long week.

Now, I don't know if that calculation of two hours of homework for every one hour of class holds true now, if it ever really did. But the fact that you should be spending significantly more time on your classes outside of the classroom than you do in the classroom is inescapable. And if you want to succeed academically without forfeiting the rest of your life, then you need to work on time management.

Some people have an innate sense of, and apparent gift for, time management. But those people are few and far between. I am not one of them, and I'd be willing to bet that most people reading this book aren't either. And even if you are someone with a natural skill for time management, you can always get even better at it.

In the Intro, I mentioned a bit about how college will likely be the first time where you haven't had a consistent daily schedule. At the same time, if you go away to school (whether you live in the dorms or off campus) it will probably be the first time you don't have a parent or someone else overseeing your schedule to some extent or another. While this near-total freedom will be liberating and empowering, it creates its own challenges. And even if you've never before had a hard time getting done the things that need to get done, college will test your limits.

One of the most certain ways to add unnecessary stress to your life (at best) or fall behind to the point of failure (at worst), is to try to do college with a "winging it" approach to time management. Playing it by ear is not a strategy at all, let alone a good one. You may be able to get by for a bit that way, but life will be so much easier and happier if you put a few time-tested tools and strategies to work.

If you take a *laissez-faire* approach to time management, what happens when this all-too-common scenario happens?

You have five classes. Three of them meet on Mondays, Wednesdays, and Fridays; the other two on Tuesdays and Thursdays. This is not a wholly uncommon schedule. Now, let's say that after your Monday classes, you don't really feel like doing a lot of homework—I mean, it's Monday, and your brain wants some rest after attending classes, and it's

Monday. Did I mention it's Monday? So you plan on doing your homework and studying for your Monday classes on Tuesday. Then, before you get a chance to do Monday's homework, you're assigned homework in your Tuesday classes that is due on Thursday. So you go home and do Monday's homework. Then you go to your Wednesday classes, go home and do Tuesday's homework. Then you go to your Thursday classes, go home and do Wednesday's homework. And so it goes for days, weeks, maybe months.

That plan may work for a while, but it's not a good long-term solution. What happens if you have a professor who, knowing you don't have her class for the next two days, decides to assign two days' worth of homework? Or when you have a huge test coming up in one of your Wednesday classes that you want to study for on Tuesday night, but you also have to get the homework done before your other Wednesday classes? Or you have a paper due on Friday that's worth 50% of your grade for the entire semester, and you need to put extra time in on it?

These scenarios are not unrealistic. If you're "strategy" for school is to get everything done the day before it's due, you're going to have a rough time. And it's going to be extremely hard to find extra time to fit in the extra studying, work on big projects, study groups, or assigned group projects in—especially if you are trying to find some time for recreation or socializing.

In the previous chapter I wrote about how confidence is the key to success, and that preparation was one of the most important ways to be confident. That concept certainly plays into time management. If you want to be ready for what college (and life) throws at you, it's best to be prepared. It's easier to adjust a plan, or fit something into a plan, when there's a plan to begin with. If your strategy is to "find time for it before it's due," and nothing more, it's not going to be easy.

What is time management?

Time management encompasses a lot more than you may think. Sure, it includes scheduling and controlling your time, but it also deals with ways to efficiently use your time and how to make time work for you. Like virtually everything that we've spoken of so far in this book, the best time-management strategy for you may look a little different from the best time-management strategy for me, or for your roommate, or your parents, or anyone else. But, also like most other things, there are certain tools and disciplines that will help you construct the best and most effective system for you. And once you've developed and started working with a time-management system, keep improving it. There will always be tools and tricks you can add to your strategy to make it even more effective.

Remember, it's not all about rigid scheduling and severe discipline to keep you on track. The best time-management strategies are flexible where they need to be and should help you manage your life, not just your academics. In fact, that's the only way it will work.

Please don't get the idea that time management means taking the fun out of your life by setting everything to a schedule and not leaving any time for spontaneity. Good time management actually allows you to be more spontaneous because you know you have enough time to get everything done, and things cropping up at the last minute won't throw such a monkey wrench into your life.

In fact, one of the keys to time management—both starting to use a time-management system and sticking to it—is to value your time. If you are able to value your time, you'll actually get more enjoyment from the time you have for recreation and socializing because you won't have to have that nagging sensation in the back of your head that you should be doing something else.

No matter how well you manage your time, other people will sometimes infringe; sometimes for good reasons, other times, not so much. But if you value your time, and show it through following a consistent time-management strategy, you'll find that you get fewer interruptions from others. When you value your time, other people will value your time, too. And if they know that you have certain time set aside for studying or homework, and other time set aside for social things and recreation, then they will be less and less likely to interrupt you when you are working. If you're consistent, you won't even feel bad about telling a friend that you can't do x right now since this is time for you to do your homework, but that you'll be able to it later (this evening, tomorrow night, whatever), because your friends will understand and begin to respect your schedule.

Practical Time Management

I've mentioned that people's time-management strategies will look different from each other's. I try to avoid referring to a "time-management system" or "time-management program" because that makes it sound like a one-size-fits-all-you-should-do-it-like-this concept; and it's not. You will find that some of the strategies I talk about in the rest of this section work better for you than others, or that you can tailor certain tools to work better for you. Go for it. You've got to figure out what is going to work for you.

Use a calendar and a planner

Or at least use a calendar that can also function as a planner. And it's probably a good idea to use a paper calendar and phone/tablet/computer, not just the electronic calendar. There are certainly benefits to using an electronic calendar, but there are also benefits to a hardcopy calendar or planner.

If you are effectively using an electronic calendar—whether Google calendar, iCal, or some other application—one benefit is that it can sync between your devices and there are options available to access it online even without your own computer or other device. You can also store a *ton* of information including notes, links, and even attachments. Another big plus is active alerts. You can set your electronic calendar to remind you when you have one week, or one day, left to finish an assignment or project, which removes even the requirement that you look at your paper calendar. And since you'll likely have your phone with you pretty much everywhere you go, you won't have to worry about taking a paper calendar or planner with you in case you need to schedule events or check on what needs to be done.

But there are also some problems you can run into if you only use an electronic calendar. One of the biggest reasons not to rely solely on an electronic calendar is the sheer amount of distractions that are also available on nearly every device from which you access the calendar. When you have some time set aside to do homework or study, and you're pulling up your calendar to check on what the assignment for your math class was, it's *really* easy to lose track of time checking your email, social networking, or even playing little games. But if you don't even need to pick up the device to check your assignment, you'll probably have an easier time avoiding those distractions.

Using a paper calendar is also effective because you can have it sitting on your desk or next to your computer (if you're working on an assignment that requires the computer) and can check it without moving to or from your work. And writing something out by hand tends to have more of an impact on mind and memory than typing something out or putting it into your phone. Taking the time to write things down will be a better reminder of what you need to do, and how much of it there is, than simply entering it into an app. And if you do both, enter it into an app *and* write it down in a hardcopy calendar or planner, then you're even more likely to remember and appreciate what's there.

Use your calendar and planner effectively

It's common time-management advice to use a calendar or a planner. Unfortunately, many advice-givers stop there. They often don't give you any tips on how to effectively use those devices. I really recognized the need for this next step not too long ago when I was looking at the planner my middle school-aged son was using to keep track of his homework. I asked him if I could see his planner. He handed it over to me, and I looked at what he had written for the day. One of the entries was: Math – HW problems.

What? That was the whole thing. I asked him what that meant, and he said he needed to do some math problems for homework. When I asked him what problems he had to do, he told me it was the problems on a certain page of his book. And when I asked him when it was due, he said, "I don't remember. I think tomorrow?"

Needless to say, although he had used his calendar, he had not done so *effectively*. And although you may be able to get away with this approach in middle school, or even

41

high school (if you have a great memory), it will be exponentially harder in college when your classes are not meeting every day, when some of the homework will not be verbally assigned, and when you will have a lot more to do.

Every time you enter an assignment into your calendar or planner, you need to include the relevant details. The most important details are exactly what needs to be done and when it is due. If you receive an assignment on a certain day, you should enter it on the day it was assigned (including the due date) and you should also enter it on the due date. When you enter it on the due date, you can enter it by either entering exactly what needs to be done once again, or by referencing the date assigned (e.g. Math 102— Assignment from 3/16 due). And if it is something that you have been given a long time to complete, you should probably enter a couple of reminders along the way so that you are getting work done on the project and not waiting until the last minute. Here's a secret: If a professor assigns you a project and gives you two weeks to complete it, she expects more than a day or two of work to go into it; and she'll probably be able to tell if you waited until the last minute.

Prioritize

Keeping a detailed calendar and planner will help you keep track of what you need to do and when you need to have it done by. But that's not enough. Time management is about more than just knowing what has to be done; it's about getting it done effectively and efficiently, with as little stress as possible.

How do you do that?

Prioritization.

Wow, that's a fun word to say: prioritization. As fun as it is to say, it's not necessarily easy to do. But if you can get good at it—you don't even have to be great—it will change your life for the better.

Priorities should be reexamined regularly and updated daily. The best way to do this is with a to-do list. You should have an updated to-do list every day. If you can color-code the list, even better. I'll give some ideas for color-coding a little later.

Choose one of two times for examining, writing, and organizing your daily list. It shouldn't take more than half an hour per day, and most days will take much less time than that. Some "experts" swear by starting each day by making your list; others say it is best to work on your list as the last part of every day, right before you go to bed. Which of these you choose doesn't really matter, but your list-work should probably be done either first or last in your day, not somewhere in the middle. This way, you have the list available to you for the whole day.

Your items should be listed by priority. The most important tasks should always be listed first. And if something has to be done by a certain time of the day, make sure that time is written on your list. If things seem to be very close priority-wise, list the hardest task first. All things being equal, you should always complete the hardest tasks—or the hardest part of each task—first. There are many reasons for this, the most important of which seem to be that the most difficult tasks seem to lead to the most procrastination, so getting them out of the way right off the bat removes some of that procrastination temptation; and, often, when the hardest part of a task is out of the way, the easier parts more or less take care of themselves.

As far as color-coding your list, you really need to find what works for you. In the past, I have color-coded my lists by when items were due; one color if it has to be done today, a different color for things that need to be finished sometime this week, and a third color for items with due-dates further out. Sometimes it makes more sense to color-code your list based upon the type of item: one color for homework, another for studying, etc.; or a different color for each subject. Find what helps you use your list most effectively, and use that method.

Scheduling

Scheduling time for things that you need to accomplish throughout your day is also important. The most effective schedules are the ones that are regular. For instance, you will do a better job making sure you have and take time for studying or homework if you use the same time every day. This also makes it easier for others to realize your schedule and, as I said earlier, respect your time.

When you schedule, it is best not to schedule *just enough* time to do the task. Things often take longer—sometimes significantly longer—than we think they will. It is also important to schedule enough time to allow for interruptions because, quite often, there will be interruptions that are beyond your control. Also, make sure to schedule some buffer time between tasks. If you've been focusing on calculus, it's going to take your brain at least a couple of minutes to switch over to the thought processes needed for psychology.

You should also schedule ample time for breaks, recreation, and socialization. And you should stick to this part of your schedule as well as you do the other parts. You'll be happy you did.

Engineering
Building successful study strategies

There's a reason I use the term "study strategies" instead of "study skills." "Skills" gives the impression that some people are just better at studying than others. But "strategies" can be used by anyone and, if used correctly, can make you successful. In fact, using study strategies will help you develop study skills.

The last chapter was, in large part, preparation for one of the most important study strategies: time management. This is the basis for studying successfully. You will remember information better, and longer, if you put it into your brain over time instead of cramming it into your head during an all-nighter. If you take the time throughout the semester to review your notes and study the class materials, you are much less likely to have to relearn everything for the final exam. If you pull an all-nighter in order to pass your first exam, you're probably going to need to learn that information again before the final, instead of just refreshing it.

To make sure you are effectively using time to study throughout the semester, you need to make sure that you schedule more out-of-class time for each subject than just what is enough to finish the homework. A benefit of homework (yes, there actually *are* some benefits) is that it helps you build and cement skills you need for the course. But homework isn't usually enough. For most courses, a professor cannot assign specific homework to cover all of the subject's contents in sufficient detail. This is where lectures and assigned reading come in. And if you want to remember what was said in lectures and reading, you'll either need to be gifted with an eidetic memory or have some good study strategies in place.

A whole book could be spent just on study strategies. I'll cover some of the basic concepts you need to know to help you start developing successful study strategies; more information is always available, and worth finding and using.

Learning to Read

Most people don't know how to read textbooks; at least, they don't know how to read them in the manner that is most effective for learning and studying. You see, reading a textbook should be a bit different from reading other types of books. It's not in your best interest to read your textbooks the same way you read novels, blogs, or the news. Most people understand that textbooks are different than other kinds of writing, and some people even try to adjust how they read textbooks. But sometimes the adjustments are counterproductive.

One of the biggest mistakes people make when they read textbooks is that the slow down and read each word carefully, trying to absorb as much information as they can as they read through the material. But a lot of the words just aren't important.

When you're reading a textbook, the first thing you should do is check for a chapter or topic summary. Many times these are at the end of chapters, but you should read it first. This will let you know what the authors, theoretically experts in the subject area, thought was most important. If you've already had a lecture on the topic, or if your professor has given you course outlines or something similar, review those before you read the whole chapter. Do this for the same reason you read the summary before you read the rest—that way you know what the experts think is the most important.

Once you've read the summary and reviewed your notes, then you should first skim through the chapter, reading as rapidly as possible to figure out the main ideas and to determine which parts you're going to want to read more carefully. Then, you read those parts more carefully to fill in the stuff you didn't know.

There's nothing wrong with reading a chapter more than once. Although some people can read a textbook chapter once and get it all, those are usually people who have some sort of background in the area, or are really interested in the subject. Most people, in most subjects, are going to need multiple readings to really understand the information.

When you are reading for a class, it is important to read actively. You've probably heard about active listening, where you don't just listen to what the other person is saying; you repeat certain things, ask relevant questions, and show that you are both paying attention and understanding what the other person is telling you. Active reading is very similar. Figure out what portions of your reading are relevant to what you're supposed to be learning. And instead of automatically rereading everything, take some time to quiz yourself on the material. Then just reread the stuff that is still confusing.

Reading textbooks, unlike reading novels, is not reading for the sake of reading; when textbooks are involved, reading is just the medium you are using to learn ideas and concepts. So most of your time spent "reading" a textbook should actually be spent making sure you have the concepts, terms, formulas, and applications down.

The nice thing about textbooks is that authors know the book is not about epic prose, that it's only real purpose is to convey the concepts about a subject to students. Because of this, authors use a bunch of different devices to make sure the most important stuff is easy to pick out. Major headings and subheadings let you know what the major points are. Bolded or italicized words or phrases will make new terms stand out. Lists are often used when enumerating things, like, "The three most important factors leading to the industrial revolution..." And then there's repetition. When points are *really* important, textbook authors will often use redundancy to show you that it is crucial to understand. If an author keeps repeating the same thing in slightly different ways, it means that the topic is a big one, and the author is hoping that one of the different phrasings will resonate with you and help you remember the idea and master the concept.

When you're reading to study, reading fast is not the most important thing. But neither is reading everything so carefully that you lose the forest of the concepts for the trees of the words. It's not about memorizing what the author says; it's about understanding the concepts.

Notes on notes

Taking notes is one of those things that nearly everybody does, but almost nobody was ever taught how to do it. And it's not something that's automatic or that everyone just knows how to do. In fact, most people probably don't take notes nearly as well as they could. It's not that hard to take good notes, you just need to know the reason and the strategy for taking notes.

You can take notes from a lecture, a study period, a class discussion, and your reading. And you should take notes on all of these. Notes from your reading may differ a little bit from the notes you take during discussions or lectures, but they still have the same end-goals and very similar strategies.

To take notes well, you need to know what notes are and, just as importantly, what notes aren't. Notes are your recordings of the main ideas and concepts. Notes *are not* a transcript of a lecture and everything the professor said. Notes should allow you to revisit the most important points of a lecture; they should not allow you the relive the entire thing. If you find yourself struggling to keep up with a lecture while you're taking notes, you should first consider whether you are taking down more than you need.

One of the easiest traps to fall into when taking notes is transcription. You start trying to write down everything the professor says, you use the professor's language, and you basically try to record everything. Two not-so-beneficial things happen when you take notes this way: 1. You don't get everything you need, because you fall behind; and 2. You don't really comprehend what the professor is saying or what you are writing because all of your concentration is spent just trying to get it down. Essentially, when you fall into transcription mode, you lose the main benefit of both the lecture and your notes.

Like a textbook, a lecture is just another medium for conveying ideas and concepts about a topic to students. Although good lectures are engaging, and even fun, lectures aren't to be consumed the same way entertainment is consumed. Most professors, like textbook authors, know lectures are for conveying ideas and educating students, and they try to make it not too hard to follow. They don't always succeed, and some even less than others, but they try.

Professors will often use the devices similar to those used by textbook authors to key you into the really important concepts. Some professors will give you outlines—these could be outlines of chapters, lectures, specific units, or even the entire course. If your professor gives you an outline, make sure you are familiar with it because it will tell you what the biggest, most important points are. If the outline is for a specific chapter or lecture, then you should know right away which concepts the professor finds most important. This is good to know because a lot of professors will test on what they think is important. Professors will often use slides of some sort, whether PowerPoint or something else, or they may write on a whiteboard (you don't see blackboards much anymore, do you?). If a professor takes the time to put something on a screen, or write it down for you mid-lecture, be sure it makes it into your notes; it's important.

Perhaps the most telltale cue a professor will use to let you know something is important is repetition. If the professor says it more than once, *make sure you've written it down at least once*, and maybe underline it. And if a professor summarizes the lecture at the end, the most important concepts and points will be part of the summary.

Another way to help you identify the most important points, and to help guide you in your note taking, is to be prepared for the lecture. If you have a professor that gives a lecture on the same things that were in the assigned reading, it can be tempting to skip the reading and just try to get everything from the lecture. This is not in your best interest. You'll get so much more out of a lecture if it's not the first exposure you've had to the material. If there is assigned reading that goes along with a lecture, do the reading. If you have the basics down before the lecture, you can use the lecture to clear up things you don't quite understand and you'll know when your professor is giving you more detail than the book on certain ideas. And, if there's a time for questions and answers, you'll know what to ask. As with so much else, preparation is key.

Practical note taking.

Now that you know what taking notes is and isn't, it's time to move onto some specific note-taking strategies. The first thing you have to decide is how you are going to take notes. And I mean this in the simplest way possible at this point: are you going to use a computer or take your notes by hand? If your school or professor does not allow you to use a computer or tablet in class, then the decision has already been made for you. But if you have the option, which do you choose?

Some people love taking notes on computers, because even average typists can type significantly faster than they can write. And if you type your notes, you never have to worry about sloppy handwriting, running out of paper, or losing your notes in a shuffle of papers. But there are significant drawbacks to using a computer for notes. When using a computer to take notes, precisely because you can type much faster than you write, it is much easier to fall into transcription mode where you are no longer engaging your brain to determine which ideas and details are the most important; instead, you are simply trying to take down everything your professor says. Although it's a nice idea to be able to write more down, it does allow you to turn off some of the listening skills that you need when you have to be more selective.

And there are some classes, some professors, and some things that simply don't lend themselves to taking notes on a computer. Illustrations, charts, and some other types of visual learning aids can be nearly impossible, and at least time-consuming, to try to put into a computer. Some of this issue can be mitigated by making sure you have a pen and paper handy, or by using certain apps or technology that allow you to handwrite as well as type into the document. But if you are switching back and forth between pen and keyboard, you will lose some of that precious speed that is the biggest benefit to using the computer anyway.

Handwritten notes can be more difficult to take because you have to be more selective, but this also helps you pay more attention to the lecture. And many people swear they remember better if they write something down by hand than if they type it onto a screen. When you take your notes the old-fashioned way, it can also be easier to find where you want to insert material if the professor goes back to something he or she said earlier. When you type, everything tends to look the same, and you don't pay attention to where on the page it is. Scrolling to find something isn't always the most efficient, and neither is cycling through all of the hits when you search within your document.

Another benefit to handwritten notes is ease of review. You don't need much space, or even electricity, to review notes you've taken by hand. And you don't get the same kind of eye-fatigue that you do from looking at a screen all the time. Much of this problem can be eliminated if you print out the notes you typed. If you plan on doing this, you should go through your typed notes, distill them down and cut out the fluff you don't need before printing them. This extra step, which includes engaging with the material to select and reformat, gives you another layer of exposure and review of the material. And it'll probably save some trees, which is nice.

Essentially, you need to find the note-taking system that works for you. It may even differ from class to class. You may find that, for you, the benefits of using a computer to take your notes outweigh the drawbacks in most classes; but for that calculus class, trying to put all of the formulas on the screen just isn't practical. And when you're deciding how you want to take notes, you need to consider how it fits into your entire study strategy. It does you no good to take better notes on your computer if you are less likely to reread and review the notes on the screen.

Some people, because repetition feeds retention, even take notes in hand during class and then transfer them to the computer as soon as possible after the class so they don't need to worry about not understanding their own hand-writing when they try to study for the exam in a couple weeks. Or you could try that strategy in reverse, taking more copious notes on your computer during class and then distilling them into writing afterward.

Some people like to record lectures. If you want to do this, there are some things you need to think about. First, some professors or institutions do not allow recording; if you plan on recording, make sure it's okay. Second, I know a few people in college and even more people in law school who recorded lectures; I know *very few, if any,* who re-listened to the lectures they recorded. Lastly, even if you have per-mission to record and you've made a practice of listening to your recordings, *never* use the fact that you're recording the lecture as an excuse for poor note taking. If you are going to use recordings, take notes while you are hearing the lec-ture for the first time and, when you re-listen to the lecture, do so with your notes in front of you, making corrections, additions, and edits to your notes as you listen to it again.

Recording lectures and using those recordings in a meaningful way is time-consuming and, for most people, not the best use of their study time. So make sure that recording is right for you before you make it the cornerstone of your study strategy.

How to take and use notes.

One of the most important things in note taking is jotting down notes in a way that helps you study from them later. Yes, this encompasses writing legibly, because you can't study what you can't read, but there is so much more to it than that. Some people do well just writing things down and reviewing them to study, but even those people could probably study a little more effectively if they put a bit more strategy into their note taking.

When you are writing your notes, don't just fill the page with writing. Be sure to leave plenty of space. This will help you revise or annotate later if you need to, and will also make it easier to read and digest the information when you're studying.

You should always review and revise your notes as soon as possible after a lecture, preferably within 24 hours. After that, you've already forgotten most, if not all, of what was actually said. And when you revise your notes, make sure you are actually doing *revision*, not just rewriting. Use revision to organize the ideas from the lecture, cut out the stuff you don't need, or even add things from the reading. You can think of the notes you took during class as your rough draft, and your revised notes as your final paper.

After you've reviewed and revised your notes, when you're studying from them, most of your time should not be spent reading and re-reading things. Instead, the great majority of your time should be spent reviewing, organizing, and testing yourself on the facts and ideas presented; mastering the formulas, technical terms, and specific things you need to know; and thinking of the applications of the ideas.

Your study time is not best used as reading time. To effectively use your study time, you should spend it learning the concepts and applications.

COMMUNICATIONS
IMPROVING YOUR WRITING

I love writing.
I love teaching writing.
I love reading writing.
I love writing so much that I wrote a book.

And because I love writing so much, and I love teaching writing so much, part of that book I wrote—the part you're reading right now—is about writing. Specifically, it's to help you improve your writing.

While it's true that some people have a gift for writing, there is absolutely no truth in the counterpoint. Everyone can become a capable writer. This is not to say that everyone can be a great writer, or that everyone has an equal chance of writing the next Great American Novel. But everyone, no matter how good they are at writing, can get better. And anyone, no matter how bad they are at writing, can become a good writer.

And becoming a good writer is as, or more, important than it ever has been, in college and in life. As technology allows more businesses to be less centrally located, it becomes more important that future employees are able to communicate in writing. And colleges are becoming more and more focused on writing, often making it an emphasis point for professors to incorporate more and more writing into their classes—everything from more papers to more writing in tests. Not to mention that professors are increasingly using essay exams because they are so much better to test students' knowledge and practical grasp of subjects as opposed to the mere recall tested in multiple choice or true-false tests.

With all the writing you'll be doing in college, and for the rest of your life, it truly behooves you to know how to do it well. And it will help you go far if you are better, or at least as good, as others; whether it's when you're looking for a higher grade or competing for a promotion. People can have the same grasp of the knowledge, but if one can communicate it better, that one will appear more intelligent. In case you haven't checked lately, it's amazing how many job postings specifically mention that they're looking for someone with "excellent written communication," and many of these are for jobs where you wouldn't think that written communication would be a necessity.

The good thing is that the increased emphasis on written communication has led to a proliferation of writing classes at colleges, and in writing instruction in non-writing classes. That said, there are many ways to make your writing even better that you are unlikely to learn even in writing classes. That said, let's get to five of the best tips to improve your writing (almost) instantly, many of which you won't hear from other places.

And if you're nice, maybe I'll give you a bonus tip.

Writing tip #5: Get (and use) a Usage Guide

Everyone knows what a dictionary is.

Almost everyone knows what a thesaurus is; some people even know how to use one effectively.

Dictionaries and thesauruses are great tools. But if I had to recommend one item that should be in every writer's toolbox, it would be a good usage guide.

The scary thing is, most people have *no idea* what a usage guide is.

So what is it?

A usage guide is a sort of super-dictionary. A really good usage guide has elements of a dictionary, a style guide, a thesaurus, a tutor, and a warm hug all rolled into one. I'll admit, I may have gone a little overboard with the "warm hug" part, but to a writing wonk like me, it's true.

Like a dictionary, a usage guide contains the definitions for many words. A usage guide won't have as many individual entries as a dictionary, and if you're just looking for what a word means, a dictionary is still your best bet. But what a usage guide does that a dictionary doesn't do, is tell you how to properly use the word; hence the name "usage guide."

And they don't stop at words. Many usage guides have entries for phrases, idioms, and even punctuation. My favorite usage guide has a long article on all of the ways to properly use a comma; it even tells you all of the ways you can use a semicolon.

I took English classes in high school and college, and I took legal writing courses in law school. Not one professor ever told me about usage guides. If more people were introduced to, and used, usage guides, their writing would be better across the board.

My favorite usage guide? For general writing, it is Bryan Garner's *Modern American Usage*. If you're looking for something specific, such as writing in a law-practice context, I highly recommend Bryan Garner's *Dictionary of Modern Legal Usage*. Both of them can be bought at Amazon.com.

Writing Tip #4: Be Consistent

This is a tip you can implement immediately but will take a lifetime to master, or at least a lot of hard work and dedication to the concept. Being consistent is valuable in every aspect of your writing. Be consistent when referencing people, places, objects, actions, or ideas; when structuring lists; and with style. And the list could go on and on.

Consistency when referring to people, places, objects, actions, or ideas can also immediately improve your writing. Implementing this tip is quite easy. By way of example, don't refer to the "letter" in one part of your document and the "correspondence" in another. If you're referring to the same object, or the same type of object, you should refer to it by the same word.[2] And if you are talking about Dr. Sam Jones, don't use Dr. Jones, Sam, Sam Jones, Dr. Sam Jones, and Jones interchangeably throughout your document. Introduce her as Dr. Sam Jones, then pick what you are going to call her for the rest of the document and stick to it. It will help, like in the list, if you choose the appropriate way to refer to Dr. Sam Jones. If you are referring to her in a way that needs the authority of her title, call her Dr. Jones; if you want to emphasize her humanity, call her Sam.

The other types of consistency we will talk about here are sometimes referred to as "parallel structure." Parallel structure is when a consistent grammatical form unites words within a sentence or paragraph.

Lists are an easy place to start practicing parallel structure. Don't make a list like this:

1. Smith letter to Jones dated February 2, 2013;
2. Photograph taken by Larkin on March 14, 2006; and
3. 5/21/08 Walker drawing.

---

[2] In this case, I would recommend using "letter." See tip #1.

Instead, make a list like one of these options:

1. February 2, 2013, Smith Letter to Jones;
2. March 14, 2006, Larkin photograph; and
3. May 21, 2008, Walker drawing.

Or:

1. Smith letter to Jones, February 2, 2013;
2. Larkin photograph, March 14, 2006; and
3. Walker drawing, May 21, 2008.

There are many options, but the key is consistency. Your list will always look and read better if you have similar items in similar places. And you can be deliberate in your consistent order. If the date is the crucial part of your list, choose something similar to option 1 above. If the creator of the item was the important part, choose something more like option 2.

But numbered and bulleted lists aren't the only places where parallel structure is helpful. Parallel structure has led to some of the most memorable passages. For instance:

> It was the best of times, it was the worst of times, I was the age of wisdom, it was the age of foolishness, I was the epoch of belief, it was the epoch of incredulity, it was the season of Light, it was the season of Darkness, it was the spring of hope, it was the winter of despair.

Even if you've never read the entire book, you probably know that this passage is the introduction to Charles Dickens's *A Tale of Two Cities*. Although we may shy away from such a long sentence, for reasons that will have to wait until another time, the power of the parallel structure is clear.

Structuring the sentence this way makes it more memorable, more powerful.

One more example, just because:

Abraham Lincoln is credited with the quote: "You can fool all the people some of the time, and some of the people all the time, but you cannot fool all the people all the time."

Honest Abe was onto something when he worded it as he did. Using parallel structure allows this concept to really hit home and makes the phrase more memorable.

Writing Tip #3: Cut "of" use by at least 25%

This is a problem faced by many. Generally, when you read a document you've written, you can safely cut your "of" use by *at least* 25%. Some, including legal writing guru Bryan Garner, recommend cutting "of" usage by at least 50%.

Why would you want to do that? Simple; "of" is often used as a crutch and props up wordy phrases that could be tightened.

One easy way to cut down on the "of" is to stop using it to show possession. Why say "the ball of John" when "John's ball" says the same thing more quickly and clearly?

You'll also find that "of" often follows or leads into a completely unnecessary phrase. For instance: Fire inspectors look at the stairways of buildings to make sure that, in case of fire, people can exit the building safely.

"Of" is unnecessary both times in the previous example. The same thing is better said, "Fire inspectors look at stairways to make sure that people can exit the building safely."

When you're done writing whatever document you're writing, go through and circle every "of." Then, look at them all and decide whether each "of" is there for a good reason; if there's no good reason for it, lose it.

Writing Tip #2: Use Active Voice

Always write in active voice unless there is a strategic reason not to. Some people have a hard time distinguishing between active and passive voice. Let's see what we can do about that.

Active voice:
The boy kicked the ball.

Passive voice:
The ball was kicked by the boy.

These examples both say the exact same thing, but one says it better and more succinctly. Using active voice helps cut unnecessary words and emphasizes the actions taken by the subject of a sentence. And it keeps the action moving. Although there is only a 2-word difference in the example's word-count, they are two words that matter. The word "by" is an unnecessary preposition that shows us that our sentence could be tightened up; and "was kicked" shows us we are not using an active verb. Any time we see "was" followed by a past-tense verb, we need to check whether we are using active voice, because we're probably not.

In active voice, the subject of the sentence takes action on the object, in that order. In passive voice, the object is acted on by the subject. When I'm teaching classes, I say, "In active voice, the subject *verbs* the object." In passive voice, the object is "*verbed by*" the subject. When you string together a few sentences, you can see the benefit of writing primarily in active voice. If you're using passive voice too often, your writing won't have that *pop*; it'll be slower and more detached.

As I mentioned at the beginning of this tip, there can be strategic reasons to use more passive voice. Some reasons for using passive voice include attempting to de-emphasize the subject or distance them from the action, or trying to slow the pace of your narrative. Just be careful not to overdo it when you strategically use passive voice; even if you are strategically using passive voice, you will not want to use it in every sentence. If you don't believe me, try it sometime. Passive voice is unwieldy, and the only strategic reason for using it in every sentence would be to make sure that no reader ever gets to the end.

Writing Tip #1: Stick with Plain English

Perchance the most ubiquitous convention ruining prose of any kind is authors' repudiation of the conventions of plain English.

Wow.

That sentence was tough to write.

And even if you didn't find it exactly difficult to read or understand, it was a lot more cumbersome than: One of the biggest problems in all types of writing is authors' refusing to use plain English.

Plain English is just what it sounds like; it's writing using plain, simple language when plain, simple language will do. It doesn't mean you never use big words or show some vocabulary, it just means using language designed to give readers the right meaning without extra effort on their part. Put simply, plain English is the rejection of "officialese" or "legalese" or an attempt to "write fancy;" if you have something to say, just say it.

Practicing law for 15 years, I have seen more than my share of documents that completely failed to use plain English. Thankfully, legal documents are getting a bit better, but they're still pretty bad. Sure, you don't see a lot of "party in the first part" and "party in the second part" in contracts anymore, but there are still a lot of wills that say, "Does hereby devise, bequeath, and bequest..." and contracts saying, "Whereas the parties are in agreement that..."

One of the biggest problems with a lot of official documents being written in this sort of hifalutin language is that readers and writers start to think official documents *need* to be written like this. It's just not true. "Devise, bequeath, and bequest" is much worse than "give;" and, "Whereas the parties are in agreement that..." is just a surplus phrase that doesn't even need to be included.

And even worse than people starting to believe that official documents need to be written in this sort of obscure language is when people begin believing that their own writing sounds more professional, more educated, or in any way better, when they start writing like this.

I really can't tell you how many times I've written, "use plain English" in red pen in the margins of student papers. A lot of students think they sound more educated or intelligent when they stuff a bunch of big words into a sentence. But in reality, it just makes the sentence harder to read and, usually, more vague.

Don't confuse keeping it simple with keeping it bland. You can write with as much, and usually more, action and intensity using plain English. Plain English allows you to keep sentences shorter, which can help your writing move faster. And you'll find that using plain English and active voice together makes your writing much more readable. And, despite what you may think, using plain English actually makes you sound smarter. This is what legal, and general, writing guru Bryan Garner says about "officialese:"

> Among the linguistically unsophisticated, puffed-up language seems more impressive. Thus, police officers never *get out of their cars*; instead, they *exit their vehicles*. They never *smell* anything; rather, they *detect it by inhalation.* They *proceed* to a *residence* and *observe* the suspect *partaking of food.* They never *arrest a person*; rather, they *apprehend an individual.* Rather than *sending* papers to each other, officials *transmit* them (by hand-delivery, not by fax). And among lawyers, rather than *suing*, one *institutes legal proceedings against* or *brings an action against.*[4]

Bonus Writing Tip: Forget what you learned in elementary school.

Okay, you've gotten this far. I guess you've earned it.

Your bonus writing tip:
Your second-grade teacher was wrong.

It is perfectly acceptable to begin sentences with "and," "but," and even "because."

"What?!" you say, "That's simply not possible! Beginning sentences with 'and' or 'but' is not allowed."

Why not?

The fact is, almost all reputable style guides permit sentences beginning with these conjunctions. And if that wasn't enough, many of the best and most well-respected writing authorities *encourage* beginning sentences, and even paragraphs, with "and" or "but."

Bryan Garner says it quite plainly, "It is rank superstition that this coordinating conjunction [and] cannot properly begin a sentence."[5] Much the same is said for beginning sentences with "but." "It is a gross canard that beginning a sentence with *but* is stylistically slipshod. In fact, doing so is highly desirable in any number of contexts, as countless stylebooks have said (many correctly pointing out that *but* is more effective than *however* at the beginning of a sentence)."[6]

But if the authorities are unified, why were you taught not to start sentences that way? I've heard some decent explanations for how this "rule" has gotten so out of hand. The most generous explanation I've heard for teaching young writers not to begin sentences with "and" or "but," is that these early writers too often start every sentence with "and." Think of a six-year-old telling a story:

> My family went on vacation. And we went the zoo. And we saw the bears. And then we went to see the alligators. And then we had ice cream. And then we went home.

Each sentence, and the entire paragraph, is grammatically correct. But it is far from elegant. One explanation, then, is that using "and" as a sentence-starter is prohibited for early writers to teach them to write with better flow.

Why, though, if that's the real reason, do so many writers get out of high school and college without ever learning that it is okay to start sentences with conjunctions?

And this is why I believe the more accurate explanation is this: the misconception that sentences cannot begin with "and" or "but" is so prevalent because students were taught this "rule" as young writers, and since they never questioned it, they went on to teach the next generation of young writers the same thing, who taught the next generation, *ad infinitum*.

A word of warning, though: you may run into a college professor or two who has yet to reach enlightenment on beginning sentences with conjunctions. If you do run into such a professor, there are a couple of options. First, if you feel comfortable and you think that the professor may be open to some learning, show the professor a copy of a style or usage guide that says such usage is allowed. Now, I recommend doing this with tact. You can say something like, "Professor, I was under the impression that it was okay to begin sentences with 'and' or 'but' because of what I read in [your resource here]." I *DO NOT* recommend going to your professor, pointing to the section of your resource that says "and" and "but" are acceptable sentence starters, and saying, "See, I was right!" or "You're wrong!"

The second option, which is just as effective and much less scary, is to just stop starting sentences with "and" and "but" when you write for that professor. Remember, right or wrong, the professor is the one who gets to grade your paper.

The Takeaway

Putting these five (plus bonus!) tips into practice will improve your writing. But don't stop here; there are so many other ways to make your writing better. You don't have to become a writing and grammar nerd like me to do it, either. There are a lot of resources out there to help you. Some resources are almost surely offered by your college, and we'll talk about some of these later in the book. Beyond that there are books, classes, seminars, and workshops that can give you guidance and help you get even better.

Writing well will get you far in college and after college. You owe it to yourself to become the best writer you can be.

ELEMENTARY EDUCATION
FINDING AND USING AVAILABLE RESOURCES

This book has been all about letting you in on some secrets, and I'm not going to stop now. This next one's a doozy, though:

Your college wants you to succeed.

Most of your professors want you to succeed.

Everyone is pulling for you.

It may be hard to believe once you hit your first round of midterms, but it is true. Other than the possibility of a couple sadistic professors out there, everyone wants you to succeed and excel at your college education. But they're not going to just give it to you. In fact, part of why it can be so hard is that your professors really want to see you succeed. And they want to do their best to prepare you to succeed in life after college.

Humor columnist and author Dave Barry once wrote:

Basically, you learn two kinds of things in college:

- *Things you will need to know later in life (2 hours)…*

- *Things you will not need to know later in life (1,998 hours)*. These are things you learn in classes whose names end in *-ology*, *-osophy*, *-istry*, *-ics*, and so on. The idea is, you memorize these things, then write them down in little exam books, then forget them. If you fail to forget them, you become a professor and have to stay in college for the rest of your life.[7]

While this is really funny and will often seem true, college is really about so much more than learning facts. And even if we narrow the discussion down to only the classroom and college academics, college is still about so much more than facts and memorization. Sure, the amount of facts you'll learn and memorize will vary depending on your major. If you're majoring in accounting, you're going to learn about—and hopefully memorize—how to do things like calculate interest and properly depreciate assets. Similarly, if you're an electric engineering major, you're going to learn about—and probably memorize—how to calculate voltage and resistance.

I majored in philosophy, so perhaps the things that Dave Barry says about forgetting the facts you learn applies more to the major I chose than it does to practical majors.[8] But for the most part, memorizing facts is just not that important in the long run. Don't use this as an excuse not to study and do well on the exam; what I mean is that, after college, you'll probably be able to look up most factual information you need. More importantly than those facts, college is teaching you how to look at and think about the things you encounter.

Let's just say you did major in electric engineering, and let's go nuts and imagine that after college you became an electric engineer. When you are asked to solve a problem as an engineer, it's unlikely to be one of the problems that you solved in class. But if you were well taught and took those lessons to heart, you're going to have a good idea at how to look at the problem and where your solution is likely to come from.

One big metaphor

Isaac Newton once wrote, "If I have seen further it is by standing on the sholders [sic] of Giants."[9] What Newton meant is that he didn't discover all of the things he discovered because he was the smartest man of all time; rather, he was able to figure out new things because of all of the discoveries that had been made before him. He didn't have to come up with everything on his own; he was able to use others' knowledge and discovery, and learn to take it further. He could see a little farther down the path, to the next discovery, because he was standing on the "shoulders of Giants," using their breakthroughs as a foundation for his own.

What you really learn in college is the foundation. Once you've learned how to look at the problem and have some idea about where the answer might be, it's up to you to build on that foundation. It's up to you to stand on the shoulders of the giants, and see just a little further. And this can be true regardless of your major or what you think of as your future career. There is always more to be learned, more to discover; better methods, more efficient processes. No matter what you do, being the best at it will always require that you learn from those who were before you, and then taking it further.

Sometimes, standing on the shoulders of the giants is difficult. I mean, it's a long climb to get all the way there. But when you're in college, it doesn't have to be as hard as a lot of people make it. Sticking with the metaphor: in college, there are people who have climbed to the shoulders of the giant before, and even if there's not, there are experts in climbing available to help you on your way.

Some people try to go it alone, free climbing all the way up (*I am really milking this metaphor*) without a rope, a harness, or any type of safety equipment. Are these the smart people? Are they the bold, or just the headstrong and rash?

You can make up your own mind about that. But know this—you don't have to make that climb alone. There are resources and tools available to help you make it. There are ways to reduce, and nearly eliminate, the danger of falling off; to help you get to the shoulders quicker, easier, and with a lot less stress.

Climbing aids

I think I'm mostly done with the climbing metaphor, but no promises.

There are so many resources and tools out there to help you succeed in college that there is no way they could all be spelled out in one book. What I'll do for the remainder of this chapter, then, is to let you know about some of the types of resources available to help you in different ways, and where you might be able to find them.

Resources at your school

Most colleges offer a ridiculous amount of services to their students. And most students never make good use of them. Not only do schools offer tons of resources, but most of them are free or extremely cheap for students. Colleges offer resources for academics, for health, for socializing, and so many other things. You have no reason to feel bad in any way about using the resources your college offers you.

One of the most underused resources that almost all colleges have is the writing center. A writing center is a place where you can receive help of one kind or another in writing papers for your classes. Writing centers are often staffed by juniors and seniors (or graduate students) who have demonstrated writing ability. Some writing centers will help you prepare to write your paper, working with you through the planning and outlining process. Perhaps the biggest value of writing centers, though, is editing. If you draft your paper with enough time to spare, you can usually take it the school's writing center and someone will go through and edit your paper to find those pesky grammatical errors, and to make sure you are communicating your ideas clearly. I cannot emphasize enough:

This.

Tool.

Is.

Invaluable.

Yet most students go through their entire college experience without ever using a writing center. No matter how good a writer you are, you can use a good editor. Trust me on this.

Even better than the writing center, sometimes you have the opportunity to get the same help from the professor who will be grading the final copy. If professors assign an extremely long paper, or a paper that is worth a large portion of your grade, they will often have interim deadlines set throughout the semester where you can turn in a draft of your paper. The professor will edit and comment on the draft, and give it back to you so you can use the edits and comments to help you in your final draft.

The last few times I offered this, I think less than 20% of my students took advantage. But the students who turned in a draft and incorporated the comments and edits into the final paper, almost always ended up with a higher final grade. Not because I was happy with them, or because I liked the fact that they had worked enough to give me a draft, and gave them a higher grade for it. No, they got higher grades because their final papers were more than what I was looking for. How could they not be? They had the benefit of a round or two of comments and edits from me; I reviewed their papers and guided them in the direction the final paper was supposed to look like.

Something you should note, though: don't just slap together something sloppy and ill-conceived and turn it in as a draft to your professor for comments. It's not going to do you much good, and it will likely make the professor less than happy if you don't spend the time making an actual, thought-through draft of your paper.

There are resources to help you with academics that go far beyond just writing help, too. Some schools offer tutoring in basic subjects for free or low cost, and even those who don't give you a price break usually have lists of qualified tutors in various subjects. It gets a little more difficult to find free tutors through the school when you get into more advanced subjects and classes, but it can never hurt to ask.

If you're having trouble with a course, contact student services and ask them what resources are available. Or you can often find resources by searching a college's web site for academic services. Your college may have a list of study groups for certain subjects. Many schools also have specific resources available to help you learn to use the technology used throughout the school. The exact type and variety of services offered will likely depend on the size and specialty of your school—a larger school will likely have more specific resources available, and a technological school that focuses on engineering will likely have more resources dedicated to math and science than sociology or philosophy.

And most schools also have specific resources available to reach your overall academic goals by helping you determine your major and other academic goals, and help you create an effective plan to get you there. This often includes scheduling your classes effectively. And if you're struggling in a class, the academic advising team is usually the best place to find specific information on all of the other services offered at your school. They can even help you find the specific resources that you need to succeed academically.

But school-supplied resources are not only about academic success. Schools offer all sorts of other services, such as counseling centers. If you feel, even in the slightest, that you could benefit from counseling, you should talk to them. If you're worried about the privacy policies, they should be able to give them to you. A nice thing about college counseling centers is they have very likely seen the problems you are facing before, and will likely have some experience helping others through the process.

Don't forget student health services. These can also be invaluable. If you think you are getting sick, call the health center and make an appointment. No use getting sicker and sicker until you have a planned visit home to see your family doctor. For illnesses and minor injuries, and often for things like flu shots and other preventive things, your college health center is the place to go. Know where it is and what services are available there. It'll likely save you some suffering at some point during your college career.

Certain issues that are faced by college students have their own support services and offices at many colleges. Women's centers are becoming more and more common on college campuses; they're there to assist and advise on issues that are more specific to female students. More colleges are also now opening offices specifically to deal with the needs and concerns of LGBTQ students.

Another concern-specific resource that is becoming more common on campuses is, unfortunately, offices and programs for survivors of sexual assault. I say unfortunately not because the resources should not be available, but because it is unfortunate that sexual assault at college is so prevalent that such resources are needed. More on this later.

Other Resources

There are many resources to help you succeed at college that are offered by the school itself. You can often find tutoring through people outside of school, but it is more useful to try to find one through the school. This is because often the tutors that you can find through your college are students who have taken the same class you are taking, from the same professor you have, and did well. While they won't be able to give you all of the correct answers to the next exam, they can give you a lot of insight about what different professors are like and what they look for in student work.

More general services are also available through services like U Ready, LLC. We are always adding new programs and resources designed to improve everyone's college experience and success. And there are other businesses around who offer tutoring and skill building in areas like time management, study skills, and even note taking.

While I certainly recommend U Ready's programs, it is more important to me that if you need tools and resources to help you succeed, you will be able to find them, wherever they are.

Reminder

Remember, even though it's sometimes hard to believe, your school and your professors want you to succeed. They want you to be a successful student. And they are willing to help you along the way, as long as you are really trying to be the best you can be.

Before you even arrive on your college campus, look around the college's website and the written materials they sent you to familiarize yourself with the tools and resources offered. Don't wait until you are really stressed out and having huge problems to start looking to see if there are any resources available. And please, don't be shy about using the resources. That's what they're there for. If the college didn't want you using the services, they wouldn't provide them.

Know where the writing center is. Learn where the health and counseling centers are. Know what services are available for the situations that could arise. You don't have to memorize every resource there is, but if you've read it and familiarized yourself with it, you'll be more likely to at least remember that there's some help out there when you begin stressing about something.

Let your college help you. They didn't let you in just for your tuition. Remember, it doesn't make the college look good to accept people and then flunk them out—colleges don't like to do that. College success is handed out or given away for free—it's not elusive or unobtainable, and your school and professors really do want to help you find it.

B.S.—
BEING SUCCESSFUL

EPISTEMOLOGY
WHAT YOU DIDN'T EVEN KNOW YOU HAD TO THINK ABOUT

Welcome to Part 3: B.S.—Being Successful. Part 2: B.A.—Basic Academics most likely dealt with things you knew you'd have to deal with when you went away to college. But there is a lot to college that you probably didn't know to expect. Nothing in this part of the book is meant to scare you away from college. Actually, nothing *anywhere* in this book is meant to scare you away from college. But I want you to be prepared, and part of being prepared is knowing what's out there.

Thinking about how you think

Socrates is known for saying that he was the smartest man in the world because he knew one thing: that he knew nothing. Socrates said that knowing that he knew nothing meant he knew one more truth than everyone else in the world. This makes great discussion for a philosophy class or a Saturday morning coffee session with friends. But if you take the statement a certain way, it's also a good starting point for getting ready to be successful at college.

If you just decide that you know nothing and think that this knowledge makes you smarter than all the other people who think they actually know things, and rest on that knowledge, then it's not helpful at all.

But, if you use that statement to constantly remind yourself that there is so much out there that you don't know, that there is always more to learn on any subject, then you can turn it into motivation to keep learning, keep preparing, and keep growing. This attitude will not only help you be as prepared as possible for college, but it will help you throughout your life. Always remember: no matter how good you are at something, you can get even better; no matter how much you know about something, you could always learn more. This attitude will keep you moving forward toward success at whatever you apply it to.

Remember, Socrates isn't one of the most influential thinkers of all time because he decided that not knowing anything made him the smartest person in the world. He is one of the most influential thinkers because he *started there*, and then he used that as a starting point to examine everything he came across. By letting go of the idea that you already know so much about something, by opening your mind and accepting that there is more to learn, you grow.

And it doesn't stop there. It's not just about knowing that there is always more to learn about things, it's also about admitting something that most people *hate* to admit.

You might be wrong.

That's a really hard truth. And I don't mean that you *are wrong*, just that you might be. A lot of people spend a lot of time going around believing they're right about everything and that everyone who doesn't agree with them is either lying, unreasonable, unintelligent, or woefully misled. You may think that accepting you might be wrong will weaken your stance on an issue, show that you're not dedicated, or diminish your credibility, but the exact opposite is actually true. Accepting that you might be wrong about something can actually strengthen your resolve. It motivates you to back up your claims, look behind them, and make sure that they have a proper foundation. And accepting that you might be wrong also *does not* mean accepting that everyone else is right. When you accept that you might be wrong, you also accept that others might be wrong. This allows you to more objectively view the basis for the things you think and believe. And if you hold a theory, belief, or idea after having viewed and weighed the evidence, after hearing both the points for and against it, then your belief will be stronger.

* * *

It's all well and good to accept that you might be wrong. So you accept it.

You begin to look at the basis and the counterarguments.

But all of the arguments against your position just seem unpersuasive, and the arguments for the position you held before are just so darn convincing.

And it's like that for everything.

You admit that you could be wrong, but it almost always turns out that you're not.

There are a lot of possibilities here, so let's look at the two most common:

Either you have the most brilliant and intuitive mind ever, which always brings you to the correct conclusions even before examining the bases for those conclusions; or,

You're human.

Humans have this interesting way of looking at the world, and it is called confirmation bias. Confirmation bias is more than just a fun phrase. Being aware of confirmation bias is the next step after accepting that no one ever knows everything about anything and accepting that you might be wrong. Confirmation bias is the tendency to search for or look at information in a way that confirms your preconceptions; put simply, it's looking at everything in a way that supports the view you already had.

You tend to look at things in a way that supports your previous views because it's easier than changing the way you look at something. I do it too. Knowing about confirmation bias doesn't completely get rid of it, but it does help us look more carefully at information; it leads us to strive for a more balanced review.

If you don't believe me, look at social networks, especially during election cycles. Everyone is, for the most part, using the exact same information and many are coming to the exact opposite conclusion. And so many people post or link to statistics or articles that they think prove, beyond question and regardless of political views, that candidate X is not fit for office. At the same time, someone else is pointing to a different article, or making a different statement based on the same facts, thinking it proves beyond question and regardless of political views that candidate X is *the only candidate* fit for office.

Or someone posts an article that points to recorded quotes from a candidate that seem damning for that candidate, and then the comment section blows up with others explaining what the candidate *really meant* or how those words, even though they were unquestionably spoken by the candidate and appear completely off-base, were actually twisted and made to look like something they weren't. And either side could be right. But both sides are convinced that, not only are they right, but that the *objective facts* are unquestionable and prove, beyond doubt, that they are right.

Confirmation bias is so prevalent in human thought that there are studies and strategies proposed to counter the effects it has on scientific experiments. Even scientists whose job it is to determine objectively whether experiments disprove or support theories fall into the trap of interpreting the evidence in a way that supports their assumptions. And if the people we've trained and trust to be objective have a hard time with it, what hope do we have for the rest of us?

Knowing that confirmation bias is a real thing, and that you—just like everyone else—lean toward it, should be enough for your day-to-day. Accepting that you tend to view information and even "cold, hard facts" through the lens of your own assumptions or preconceived notions allows you to at least try to take a more objective look at the information and make a decision based on it.

How to find the answers

One of the most important lessons you'll learn in life is that, often, knowing how and where to find the answers is just as important as knowing the answer. And you should know that people usually respect that. If you tell someone that you don't know the answer off-hand, but you have some ideas and know how to find the answer, that's almost always good enough. But don't try to use that on an exam paper. Although your professor may appreciate that you've at least learned where to go for the answer, it's not likely to get you points on the exam.

They gave you that stuff for a reason

One of the things I started noticing, before I was even accepted to college, was how much paper colleges use. While more stuff is done online now than it was... not *that* long ago, colleges still use a lot of paper. And if they're not using paper, they're blowing up your inbox with information.

And, oddly enough, a good amount of it is actually important.

Important enough that you should probably read it.

If you're anything like me, you get a ton of information thrown at you daily. Whether it's email, social networking information, private messages, texts, or even physical mail; a lot of it goes straight to the trash or the recycling bin—both physical and virtual. There are even a bunch of people or companies who send me stuff that I get rid of without even seeing what the item is specifically about.

Don't do that with stuff from your school.

Once you are accepted to a school, it's important to at least know what the communication is really about before you delete it. And you may not always be able to tell from the subject line, so at least skim everything the school sends you. That will make you much less likely to miss anything important.

And don't give anything the TL,DR (too long, didn't read) treatment. A lot of the longer things you receive will be the most important. Take, for instance, the student handbook. This is a document you should at least quickly read *in its entirety*. Even if the school doesn't send you a paper copy or an electronic document, you can usually find it online, and they've probably at least given you a link to it.

Unless you're one of the rare few, you probably made it through high school without ever reading through the student handbook. And yes, your school *did* have one. But college is a different animal altogether. The student handbook provides all sorts of important information, including most of the school's rules; how the school defines things like academic dishonesty, plagiarism, hazing, sexual assault, and many others; how to address grievances with professors or other students; emergency procedures, and other things.

The student handbook, or other documents provided in what many schools call the "welcome packet," may also tell you whether, by signing the line and agreeing to attend that particular school, you've agreed that any school-based counseling notes or academic records are accessible by your parents; or whether you've agreed to abide by the school's rules when you're off campus (often even when you're on school breaks, including summer break). These are things you should know, especially if you attend a school that has rules governing a lot of social interaction.

You don't want to be surprised by being called into a disciplinary hearing when you did something while you were home over summer break that was against your school's code of conduct.

* * *

Another thing your college gave you for a reason is your school email address. You certainly don't need to use it for all of your personal correspondence, but you better check it daily or have it set up to forward all of your email to whatever account you do check. Although some professors may ask students for their preferred email addresses, many will use the list of email addresses provided by the college on their class lists, which will be your school-assigned email. This is also the email address that the college will use for their official communications with students, whether communication specifically to you or school-wide email blasts. If the school gave you a method of communication, the school expects to be able to communicate with you via that method. It's kind of like that lecture you got from your parents the first time they couldn't get ahold of you on your cell phone, and probably the second and third time, too.

Safety first

Your college will also provide you information about safety procedures. Sometimes this includes the recommended way to handle different sorts of events, like when you notice someone in psychological crisis. But it will also include information about how you will be warned of dangerous situations on campus.

* * *

There is another piece of information that you should see. Your college probably doesn't send you this document, and sometimes it's a trick to find it on a school's website. But, by law, your college, unless it is one of the handful of private schools that does not accept any federal funding, is required to compile and share information about crime on campus and the school's efforts to improve campus safety. Colleges are also required to inform the public about crime in or around campus. According to law, *this information must be publicly accessible.*

The report of crimes on or around campus is one of the many requirements of the *Clery Act*.[10] The Clery Act is one of the most important laws when it comes to campus safety. There are some portions of the Clery Act that I will discuss in more detail in Chapter 11—Sexual Education, but much of the act is important for general college safety as well.

Under the Clery Act, colleges are required to provide an annual security report by October 1 of each year. And this report must be given to all current students and employees, with a direct link to the report, so no one has to search for it. Schools are also supposed to give information about the annual security report, including how to access the report, to prospective students. The annual security report will include crime statistics for the campus and surrounding areas, with breakdowns of the type or crime and the general location. Along with the statistics, colleges should use the annual security report to tell people about their campus safety and security efforts.[11]

* * *

The Clery Act also requires ongoing reporting by colleges. This means that, if and when an incident happens, the college has to determine if an emergency notification or a timely warning needs to be given to the campus community; and the school must have policies for both emergency notifications and timely warnings.

Most colleges now have text-alert systems, and virtually all will also provide alerts via email to that college-assigned address unless your school allows you to opt in to the system with a different email address. If your college has a text-alert system, make sure you're signed up for it with your own cell number. If the horrible situation of a school shooter occurs at your school, the text-alert system is the best way to be informed about that danger.

* * *

Colleges will provide text alerts and emails about other things, too, like whether classes are cancelled because of weather (it's a real issue in some places).

And if extreme weather, like tornadoes and hurricanes, is a real possibility at your college, make sure you know what the appropriate precautions are. Are there certain buildings or areas of buildings on campus that are to be used for tornado or hurricane shelter? Probably. And if so, your college has probably already given you that information before you set foot on campus.

Be sure you know how your school is going to communicate with you. And make sure you get the message and read it.

* * *

Most schools now have some program or another that makes it so students do not have to walk alone at night. Often this will include rides or walks with police or campus safety personnel, or it may be a group on campus that arranges times for people to travel together so no one is walking alone. There is just no reason not to make use of these safety programs if you're not out with friends. If nothing else, it will make you feel safer as you walk around after dark.

The other stuff to think about

There are a bunch of other things that you'll want to think about before you go to college, too. But I'm not going to talk to you in depth about those things now. For instance, laundry—you should know how to do your own laundry and where to do it. You should have at least a rudimentary grasp of how to eat healthy and exercise. If you're adventurous, it's worthwhile to learn how to cook at least a few simple meals—for when you move off-campus and away from the dining halls—and even how to iron your clothes if you don't know already.

In fact, there are a lot of everyday tasks that you may not know how to do. But I'm sure you'll be able to find the answers and figure it all out. Remember, there's always more to learn.

And hey, if you're too embarrassed to ask your parents whether you should put that sweater in the dryer, I guess you can always Google it.

HOSPITALITY
FRIENDS AND SOCIALIZING

Going away to college comes with so many opportunities: there's more freedom; the opportunity for a great education followed by a fantastic job; and networking and meeting a new group of friends, which I'll discuss in a bit. But one of the first opportunities you have when you go away to college is the opportunity to reinvent yourself.

The chance for a new you.

The opportunity to have the image you've always wanted.

The possibility of changing your social status and be a part of that group that you always thought you belonged with in high school, but were never able to break in to.

The chance to shape a completely different persona than the one you were stuck with in the past.

If this is something you're interested in doing, my advice can be boiled down to two words:

BE CAREFUL.

I don't mean be careful your past stays your past. I don't mean be careful to separate your new friends from the old so that your high school persona doesn't come crashing in on your college persona. And I certainly don't mean to be careful to avoid the people at your college who knew you in high school.

What I do mean is more akin to: be careful what you wish for.

Be careful not to alienate yourself from yourself.

Be careful not to turn yourself into something you're not for the sake of popularity, promise of future opportunity, to impress your new friends, or to gain the interest of the significant other of your dreams.

Becoming who you "really are" is one thing. If you needed the freedom of being away from the people who've known you since you were young, or the freedom to discover who you really are away from all the people who have been telling you who you are or who you should be your whole life, then that's a good thing. Sometimes we need to get away from the voices of our past influences to *realize* who we really are.

But trying to *change* who you really are is another thing altogether. If you're unhappy with your life or your high school experience; if you've seen the lives of others from the outside and determined that your life would be better if you were more like them; and you decided that when you "get away from it all," you're going to change yourself into that...

BE CAREFUL.

The only saying, "Wherever you go, there you are," may be trite and clichéd, but it's also true. The worst thing you can do to yourself is to try to be something other than what you are.

Please, please, please, don't take this the wrong way. I am not trying to say that you can't change yourself or better yourself. If you think you would be happier, inside and out, if you hung out with a different group of friends, or even if you dressed a different way, it's not wrong to make those changes. But be sure you're making them for the right reasons. Be sure you're making them to be true to yourself.

I've seen too many times when young people who were really good students, some might have called them "nerds" in high school, went away to college and tried to change their image. They decided that when they got to college, they would do whatever was needed to be part of the crowd they thought was cool. It seldom ended well.

Yes, there can be a bunch of changes you want to undertake to make yourself a better version of you—just make sure that it's really a version *of you*.

The changes that you want to make are the ones that reject the negative voices that you've heard and the lies about yourself that you may have bought into. If you've always been told, by yourself or someone else, that you're not good enough, that you aren't smart enough to excel at college; and if you've made "not smart enough" part of you, *change that*. It's just not true. If you've been told that you don't have the skills or abilities to make yourself better, and if that has become part of who you are, *change that*. These are the things that you really want to change.

Trying to be someone you're not won't solve your problems, change all of your external circumstances or surroundings, and it will not make you happy. Wherever you go, there you are. But if you change your external circumstances or surroundings because of who you are, it may make you happier. This may be a fine line, and it's probably easy to end up on the wrong side of it.

Be you, whatever that may be.

You'll be happier for it.

Friends

While some students who go away to college end up at the same college with a bunch of their high school friends, most probably don't. This was certainly my experience. I think there was only one girl from my high school graduating class that went to the same college I did. My high school's graduating class was around 700, and the school I went away to was only about 2 ½ hours from my hometown, and in the same state. And, with that class of around 700, she and I weren't that close in high school, and I don't think we socialized at all in college.

That said, when I went away to college, I had to make a whole new set of friends. And although it was scary in the beginning, it all turned out okay. I made it through. And this was before Facebook and other social networking applications made it easy to stay in touch with all of your friends no matter where they went to school. I don't want you to tune out whatever else I say after this, but I even went to college before everybody had a cell phone.

Still, I made some friends. I may have never been the most popular guy at school, but that was never my goal. What I did have was a group of close friends and a larger group of more casual friends who I could hang out with and talk to. They were real friends. I kept some of my best friendships from high school, and still do to this day. But I had friends in college, and still have some of those friendships, too.

One of the most important pieces of advice about having meaningful friendships in college is the advice your parents or grandparents probably told you in the past: be yourself. But I don't want to dwell on the things you've heard a million times.

In the college context, it's important to mingle a bit. Don't latch on to a group of friends as soon as you move into the dorms and then never expand your circle. This can lead to a lot of problems. You don't want to end up in a group of people who you know aren't good for you, but feel like you'll be without friends for the rest of your college career if you walk away from that group. I'll talk about this a little in the next chapter in the context of hazing.

Sure, there'll probably be a group of people that you relate with more than others, but don't limit yourself to only talking or hanging out with that group. And just because you're friends with someone, or a group of people, doesn't mean you have to do everything they do. If you've got a friend in your dorm who invites you to go with them to an orchestra concert, but you hate classical music, you've no more or less obligation to go there than to the fraternity party your roommate invited you to.

You will often hear that college is a time of growth and experimentation. And there is truth to this. But not all experimentation is good experimentation. Like I said about using college as your chance to become a different person: be careful. Remember, not everything that happens in college stays in college. Good reputations can be shattered by one mistake or wrong action, and lives can forever be altered. I'm not trying to scare you, but you do need to know that even the things you do in college have consequences.

Alcohol

One thing that you need to be careful with is alcohol. It seems to be nearly ubiquitous on some campuses, and it is seemingly present on nearly all of them, even the "dry" schools where alcohol is not permitted.

I'm not here to tell you what to think about drinking in general. You already have opinions about that, and there's no doubt in my mind that you know the legal drinking age. But there are some things you need to know about drinking in college.

First, studies show that college students drink more than people the same age who are not in college. According to 2014 numbers, 59.8% of full-time college students ages 18-22 drank alcohol in the past month compared with 51.5% of other people the same age.[12] The numbers of college students engaging in binge drinking, defined as five or more drinks on a single occasion, and heavy drinking, defined as five or more drinks on an occasion on five or more occasions per month, are also higher for college students ages 18-22 than for non-college students that are the same age.[13]

There are, of course, consequences for this type of drinking behavior. According to the National Institute on Alcohol Abuse and Alcoholism, researchers estimate that each year:

- 1,825 college students between the ages of 18 and 24 die from alcohol-related unintentional injuries, including motor-vehicle crashes.[14]

- 696,000 students between the ages of 18 and 24 are assaulted by another student who has been drinking.[15]

- 97,000 students between the ages of 18 and 24 report experiencing alcohol-related sexual assault or date rape.[16]

- Roughly 20 percent of college students meet the criteria for an AUD [alcohol use disorder].[17]

- About 1 in 4 students report academic consequences from drinking, including missing class, falling behind in class, doing poorly on exams or papers, and receiving lower grades overall.[18]

Those numbers are big.

So, yeah, drinking responsibly is really important. And it's important to look out for other people, too. Don't let your friends do stupid things when they're drunk, and ask them not to let you do stupid things if you're drunk.

And this is without going into the standard advice. If you're going to drink, know what you're drinking and be aware of how much. Don't let other people just continually fill your glass. It's safer to drink out of cans or bottles of things you brought and opened yourself. Also, don't leave your drink unattended.

If you're going to go out or go to a party, go with friends you can trust and make a deal to watch out for each other. Let your friends know where you're going and what you're planning on doing, so they can look out for you. If you're going to a party and you know you don't want to "hook up" with anyone, tell the friends you're going with, and tell them to make sure you don't. You shouldn't have to protect yourself from predators who will incapacitate you and then take advantage, but the truth is, they're out there.

Drunk or Dying? You make the call.[19]

When a large part of my law practice was representing the families of victims of school violence and hazing, one disturbing thing I saw repeatedly was students who died from alcohol poisoning—especially when they were dying while others left them to "sleep it off." Sometimes letting someone sleep it off included relatively routine checks to make sure the person was breathing or had a pulse.

As a general rule, if someone is to the point where you feel the need to check their pulse or breathing because you know they're in danger of either of those not being present, *you need to get them medical help. IMMEDIATELY!*

Aware Awake Alive, an organization dedicated to preventing loss of life from alcohol poisoning, has coined a great mnemonic for teaching the symptoms of alcohol poisoning. The phrase to remember is "MUST HELP."[20]

- **M**: Mental Confusion
- **U**: Unresponsive
- **S**: Snoring/Gasping for Air
- **T**: Throwing Up
- **H**: Hypothermia
- **E**: Erratic Breathing
- **L**: Loss of Consciousness
- **P**: Paleness/Blueness of Skin

What do you do when you see signs of alcohol poisoning? Never assume someone will "sleep it off;" even when someone has stopped drinking, alcohol continues entering the bloodstream and the blood-alcohol content continues to rise. If a person is unconscious, breathing less than eight times per minute, or has repeated, uncontrolled vomiting, call 911 immediately.

If the person is conscious, call the poison control center (800-222-1222 in the United States, you'll be routed to your local center); the staff there can tell you whether you should go directly to the hospital. Calls to poison control centers are confidential.

Whoever you call, be ready to provide information. If you can, tell the hospital or emergency personnel what and how much the person was drinking, and when. Don't ever leave an unconscious person alone, and while you're waiting for help, don't try to make someone vomit. Alcohol poisoning affects the gag reflex; someone with alcohol poisoning could choke on his or her vomit or accidentally inhale vomit into the lungs, which can cause fatal lung injuries.

Remember, out of those 1,825 alcohol-related deaths of college students each year, more than a few are alcohol-poisoning deaths. Many alcohol-poisoning deaths can be prevented if you can recognize the signs and if you know what to do.

And most colleges now have amnesty policies, meaning that if you call for help when someone is in danger because of alcohol or drugs, you won't get in trouble from your school if you've been drinking. You can check your student handbook to see if your college has an amnesty policy. But even if your school doesn't have amnesty for people seeking medical help for others, don't you think you'd rather get in a bit of trouble for drinking than have someone die when you know you could have saved them?

If you can't tell if they're drunk or dying, *you make the call*.

PSYCHOLOGY
HAZING

Hazing.
What is it?
Why do you care?
Do you *really need* to know more about hazing?
Hazing has been in the national spotlight for the past few years, and the general public is starting to see more of the dangers caused by it. But hazing is not a *new* problem. Hazing—even the dangerous, sometimes deadly hazing you hear about in the news—has been going on for a very long time. And I'm not just talking about decades here; I'm talking about over a century.

It is commonly accepted in the fraternity industry, and among hazing experts, that there has been at least one death in the United States each year since 1970 as a result of hazing. Although there are no official statistics on hazing, hazing expert and author Hank Nuwer has compiled a list of hazing deaths; his first entry is from 1838 and the most recent, confirmed hazing death is from 2014 (with deaths in 2015 and 2016 that have alleged hazing links).[21]

The first anti-hazing law, New York State's, was put on the books more than 120 years ago.[22] Now, 44 states have their own anti-hazing laws. Every state except Alaska, Hawaii,

Montana, New Mexico, South Dakota, and Wyoming, specifically outlaws hazing itself. And of the six that don't, one of the primary reasons many of them haven't passed an anti-hazing law is that lawmakers say hazing is already covered under other laws like assault, battery, or others.

Following the brutal hazing-related death of Robert Champion at Florida A & M University, Florida Congresswoman Frederica Wilson began stumping for a federal law against hazing in late 2011. To date, no federal anti-hazing legislation has been enacted, and hazing is likely to remain in the hands of individual states for the foreseeable future.

The problem with having 44 different states with 44 different laws against hazing is that they do not all have the same definition or consequences. They have not all agreed on whether hazing is a misdemeanor or a felony, or even who is ultimately responsible for hazing—is it the organization? The individuals involved in the hazing? Both?

The common definition I will use for hazing is the one used in the most recent national study of hazing, the findings of which were published in 2008. Hazing was defined as "any activity expected of someone joining or participating in a group that humiliates, degrades, abuses, or endangers them regardless of a person's willingness to participate."[2324]

There are three main parts of this definition you should be aware of to really understand hazing:

- Any activity expected of someone joining or participating in a group;

- When the activity humiliates, degrades, abuses, or endangers that person;

- Regardless of the person's willingness to participate in the activity.

Each of these parts is crucial to a full understanding of hazing, why it persists, and its destructive nature.

Any activity expected of someone joining or participating in a group

Hazing is always done in conjunction with a group of people. It does not necessarily have to be a formally recognized group or an established entity. If there are "rites of passage" or "initiation activities" that are required to become part of a group, it could be hazing. This is not to say that every initiation activity is hazing. For instance, filling out new-member paperwork is much less likely to be hazing than other activities. But if the paperwork requires you to identify your most embarrassing moment in life, it may well cross the line.

In short, to be hazing, the activity in question must be required for someone to either join or participate in a group. Most people seem to understand that hazing happens to people trying to join a group; fewer understand that someone who is already part of a group can still be hazed. If activities are required for a person to participate or remain a member of a group, they could be hazing. Just because someone has already been accepted into a group does not mean that the person can no longer be hazed.

The type of group you most likely connect to hazing is college fraternities. Hazing also occurs in sororities; collegiate athletics; collegiate bands, orchestras, and performance groups; club sports; intramural sports; cultural and interest clubs; and many other groups.

When you think of hazing, you probably think of fraternities or sororities. And although the national or international bodies of all of the major fraternities have expressly forbidden hazing in their fraternity rules, it still takes place at countless local chapters. But hazing is not solely a fraternity problem; the National Study of Student Hazing found that 55% of college students involved in clubs, teams, and organizations experienced hazing.[25] This means that *regardless of the type of group joined*, more than half of college students involved in extracurricular collegiate activities are hazed. According to the study,

> Students report experiencing hazing behaviors across a range of group-types including athletic teams and Greek-letter groups as well as club sports, intramurals, performing arts groups, service fraternities and sororities, recreation clubs, honor societies; and some students indicated they had experienced hazing in other kinds of groups as well including military groups, religious or church-based groups, student government, and culturally-based student organizations.[26]

This shouldn't be a deterrent to joining a student group, but it should cause you to be wary. If you have to put yourself through a horrible or negative experience, or engage in actions you would otherwise stay far away from, do you really need or want to be part of that group?

When the activity humiliates, degrades, abuses, or endangers that person

Not all activities are hazing. Only those that cause or are likely to cause physical, mental, or emotional harm to the person trying to join the group. Although 1978's *Animal House* certainly showed a bunch of hazing activities, it played them for laughs and never showed the all-too-real dangers of the activities.

You may think the paddling scenes in movies or television shows where people try to join fraternities are just jokes and aren't real. If you thought that, you'd be wrong. Many fraternity and sorority chapters throughout the United States still use paddling or similar physical-abuse activities as part of their pledge or initiation rituals. And, again, this is not limited to Greek-letter societies. The death of Robert Champion, mentioned earlier, was part of a hazing ritual for people involved in the university's marching band. Champion, newly promoted to drum major, was required to "run the gauntlet," going up and down the aisle of one of the marching band's busses while other band members tripped, punched, kicked, choked, and hit him with objects. This physical abuse killed Robert Champion.

And he's not the only person who has died from this type of hazing.

One type of hazing that is often overlooked by the public, or not understood by many students to be hazing, is participation in drinking games or rituals. In past years, this type of hazing has caused multiple deaths. From students being required to finish a bottle of their "family drink" in a certain amount of time; to a group of pledges (the people trying to join an organization) being locked into a room with copious amounts of alcohol and told none of them can leave the room until they drink all of the alcohol; to new members being given a bag or box filled with various alcoholic drinks and told to drink them by a certain time. Alcohol-based hazing rituals are, sadly, common.

Dave Westol, former CEO of Theta Chi Fraternity, talks specifically about the use of alcohol in hazing and its horrible consequences, in his article, *The Three Deadly Nights*.[27] Westol details three traditional nights—bid night, big brother/sister night, and pre-initiation—that take place in many hazing groups, when the risk of death-by-alcohol is greatly increased. If you look at Hank Nuwer's list of hazing deaths that I mentioned earlier, you'll be shocked by the number of alcohol-related deaths.

But it's not all beatings and alcohol. According to the Allan/Madden Study, "Alcohol consumption, humiliation, isolation, sleep-deprivation, and sex acts are hazing practices common across types of student groups."[28] Yes, you read that right: humiliation, isolation, sleep-deprivation, and sex acts. Prisoners at Guantanamo Bay were subjected to these same acts (although sometimes, but not always, more extreme versions) according to the "Torture Report" unclassified by the government in 2014.[29] If a version of it is considered torture, then it's not worth doing it to be part of a group at college, or anywhere.

During hazing, humiliation might include wearing clothes or costumes one wouldn't otherwise wear; being called exclusively by a vulgar or degrading nickname or label; being required to perform, sing, or chant in front of people; and many other things.

Isolation can happen to individuals or, sometimes, to the entire group of prospective members. This could include a broad isolation, like not allowing prospective members to speak with anyone outside the group; or direct isolation, like locking prospective members into small, dark rooms for long periods.

Hazing involving sleep-deprivation may include a bunch of activities taking place at night; waking up in the early morning for activities; actually putting potential members in a room with group members taking shifts making sure potential members don't sleep; or calls and texts throughout the night requiring prospective members to participate in tasks or run errands for members.

Hazing through sex acts can involve a multitude of activities. It could include requiring a potential member to have sex with someone from another group; it could involve masturbation; strip shows; prospective members being violated with objects; or numerous other lewd or humiliating sexual acts.

Don't get the wrong impression. There are groups where none of these things take place. But don't think that it could never happen in the group you want to be part of. The fact is, it could, and you should be prepared to walk away from groups who ask you to submit yourself to hazing. And know this, if you suffer through the process to become a member yourself, the next time someone new wants to join, you'll be asked (read: required) to put them through it, too.

Regardless of the person's willingness to participate in the activity

This is the part of the hazing definition that sometimes trips people up. It's really easy to say, "Nobody held a gun to his head," or "He didn't have to stay." but there is a lot of psychology at work in hazing situations. Westol puts it this way when describing the Three Deadly Nights:

> And yes, we've heard all of the excuses and tortured rationalizations about new members or pledges consuming alcohol within the context of bid night. They come in many different forms from many different people. "They didn't have to drink." "We drank with them." "No one forced them to drink." "It was their choice." "Some guys didn't drink at all."

*   *   *

> The fact is that new members or pledges do not have a choice...not if they want to be accepted...not if they

want to be part of the brotherhood...not if they want to demonstrate that they truly belong.[30]

Almost every college specifically says in its rules against hazing that consent by the person being hazed does not remove the hazers' liability. Many state anti-hazing laws also include that consent of the hazed does not relieve hazers' liability. What this means is that it doesn't matter whether someone trying to join an organization agrees to be hazed, it is still against the rules—and often the law—to haze.

There are some good reasons for this rule. There is a lot of peer pressure involved in hazing. And even if unintentional, the way many hazing organizations work magnifies that pressure. A lot of these organizations start recruiting members as soon as new students set foot on campus. And because there are so many events and get-togethers during the joining process, the prospective new member doesn't have any friends at college outside of the organization. This is sometimes compounded by hazing groups that don't allow new members to socialize outside the group.

If someone is new on campus, and their only friends are part of an organization, there will be much more pressure for them to go along with hazing "willingly" for fear that if they walk away, they will be rejected by the group and left friendless for the rest of college. While it is unlikely that anyone would actually end up friendless throughout college, if someone's identity has become so wrapped up in the group they want to be part of, it's easy to think this way. And even if backing down would not cause the potential member to be excluded from the group, the potential member could justifiably think that they will be thought of as weak or less of a member. Coercion and groupthink can be powerful forces. When considering a case involving a hazing death, the Maryland Court of Appeals said it very well:

The power of peer pressure cannot be emphasized enough. Students willingly subject themselves to these acts to be accepted. Many times they have no idea of how bad the hazing will be until they are put in the situation. By then, it is too late and they accept the consequences rather than "lose face" by backing out.[31]

And this is where the problem *always* lies. Hazers may say, "She could have left whenever she wanted," or "He didn't have to do it, we didn't *force* him," but the reality is, while the person being hazed may have technically been able to leave at any time, the hazers and the hazing put them in a position where that decision is almost impossible.

The argument that the person being hazed underwent the hazing voluntarily is also belied by the way hazing most often takes place. You're right, there's a good chance that if some extreme hazing took place right off the bat, more people would leave instead of being hazed. But the hazing usually starts off with something fun, or something that might be a little weird but is pretty harmless. Then, over time, the hazing progresses until it gets to a point where the person being hazed has already gone through enough that they'll want to complete the process, because otherwise it will be all for nothing.

Why does it matter?

It's important to know what hazing is. Not only should you know when lines are being crossed, you should know how to talk and think about hazing intelligently. When you see or hear about something that looks like hazing, never accept the "she did it voluntarily" or "he could've left whenever he wanted" excuse. And don't accept it from the person being hazed either; don't let someone who is being hazed tell you, "It's okay, I'm good with it."

Remember that hazing has an effect on people. There are a bunch of psychological reasons why someone will be "willing" to go through with being hazed. And there are reasons your college's rules, and the rules of most organizations, specifically prohibit hazing and say that hazers will be punished even if the person being hazed was willing to participate.

Hazing is pervasive in the culture of many student groups. It is so pervasive that even laws and college or group rules are not enough to stamp it out. And although there is an air of secrecy to hazing and group rituals, the National Study on Hazing tells us that it's not just sneaky students who haze or allow hazing to exist. According to the study:

- In 25% of hazing experiences, students believed coaches and/or advisors were aware of the activities.

- In 25% of hazing experiences, students reported that alumni were present.

- Students are most inclined to talk with peers (48%, 41%) or family (26%) about their hazing experiences.[32]

You need to know these things so you can protect yourself and others from hazing. You need to know so you can have all the available information you need before you join an organization. Know this: asking someone who is already part of the group you want to join may not give you a full answer about the group's hazing practices. But chances are, if the group hazes, someone knows about it, and the information is likely out there to be had.

"But it's not really hazing," or "It's not really so bad"

We mentioned some of the things said by those trying to excuse their own hazing behavior. The National Hazing Study reports that there is a gap between students who experience hazing and their willingness to call it hazing; "Of students who report experiencing a hazing behavior in college, 9 out of 10 do not consider themselves to have been hazed."[33]

This is because some students identify hazing with physical force like paddling or beating, and many others think that hazing is an activity that must be against the will of a person. Many believe this even though their school or a national organization/association hold a different position.[34]

And just because others went through it in the past doesn't make it okay, either. When one person trying to join an organization dies from the liquor new members have to drink while they're locked in a room, does it matter that the 10 people seeking membership last year are still all alive?

There is nothing accomplished by hazing that cannot be accomplished in other ways. Many groups and organizations throughout history have built group unity and a sense of accomplishment without hazing.

*   *   *

Remember, it's never okay to haze. And no one has the right to haze you as part of your initiation or introduction to an organization. In most states, it's against the law. At nearly all schools, it's prohibited and can lead to strict punishments for the people who haze. And hazing doesn't make any organization stronger or more exclusive. Don't become part of the tradition of hazing. It literally kills people every year, and harms many more along the way.

You deserve better than to be treated like that. If you find yourself in a situation where someone is hazing you—and if you ever have to ask the question, "Is this hazing?" then it is—don't accept it. Report it. Protecting yourself and others from harm is *much* more important that protecting the reputation of the group.

SEX EDUCATION
THE REALITY OF SEXUAL ASSAULT

S exual assault at colleges has been even bigger news than hazing over the last few years. And all sides have been hit. Sometimes it's hard to know what to believe about it. People quote studies saying one thing, then someone else tells you that those aren't "real numbers," and another person tells you that it's mostly made up.

Let's get some things straight right off the bat:

- Sexual assault is real.

- Sexual assaults really happen at colleges and universities.

- They happen in troubling, if not epidemic numbers.

- Almost no one knows how to talk about sexual assault in a meaningful or helpful way.

- Sexual assault survivors are real people, who deserve to be treated appropriately.

If that wasn't enough to get your attention:

- No one ever has a right to another person's body.

- No one ever "asks" to be sexually assaulted; and no one ever "had it coming."
- Nothing you do ever entitles you to sex.
- Nothing anyone ever does to or for you ever entitles them to sex with you.

Many of these things will be discussed more thoroughly in this chapter, but we needed to have a strong starting point.

Sexual assault is a difficult topic to discuss. Chances are, you come to the discussion with certain preconceived notions—some of which may be correct, while others may be incorrect. And there's also a chance that you feel strongly one way or the other about how college sexual assault has been handled by the media and by colleges and universities. Not to mention the fact that it's just a difficult topic to discuss, anyway. Sexual assault, including rape, deals with one of the most, if not *the most*, severe violations of a person.

Not one study, but several studies over the last few decades have consistently found that 20-25% of college women are victims of attempted or completed nonconsensual sex while in college.[35]

Women are the targets of 91% of rapes and sexual assaults, with 9% targeting men.[36]

Less than 5% of attempted and completed rapes are reported to police or other law enforcement.[37]

Sexual assaults happen most often when college women are the most vulnerable: during their first two years in college, and often during their first week on campus.[38] And most sexual assaults happen "when college women are alone with a man they know, at night, and in the privacy of a residence."[39]

Title IX and sexual discrimination, harassment, and violence

One of the most important laws governing sexual discrimination, harassment, and violence at colleges and universities is Title IX. Title IX, more formally 20 U.S.C. §1981 *et. seq.* or Title IX of the Education Amendments of 1972, deals with sex discrimination and harassment of students. Under Title IX, "No person in the United States shall, on the basis of sex, be excluded from participation in, be denied the benefits of, or be subjected to discrimination under any education program or activity receiving Federal financial assistance."[40]

Many people know Title IX mostly from its application to athletics, where it has been used to increase athletic opportunities for women. And although Title IX has been instrumental in this area, it is about so much more than sports.

Title IX covers sexual harassment, gender-based discrimination, and sexual violence. Sexual violence is not limited to completed rape or sexual assault; it includes attempted rape and sexual assault, sexual harassment, stalking, voyeurism, exhibitionism, verbal or physical threats or abuse based on sexuality, and intimate partner violence. And unlike some people believe, Title IX does not only apply to women, it protects *everyone* from sex-based discrimination "regardless of their real or perceived sex, gender identity, and/or gender expression. Female, male, and gender non-conforming students, faculty, and staff are protected from any sex-based discrimination, harassment or violence."[41]

Schools have to do more than react to claims of sexual violence or discrimination after they happen; they have to be proactive to ensure students a campus free of sex-based discrimination. The Department of Education's Office of Civil

Rights—often called "the OCR"—and courts throughout the country have made it clear that Title IX also covers peer-to-peer sexual violence. This means that your college or university does not only have to make sure that they are not discriminatory in their programs, but they are also responsible for sexual violence and discrimination *by students against students.*

One of the things Title IX requires colleges to do is establish a procedure for handling complaints of sexual discrimination, harassment, or violence. Schools' procedures for handling these complaints are usually different than the procedures for handling other types of complaints. You should familiarize yourself with your school's procedures, and have at least a general idea of how your school handles these claims, which will allow you to help yourself or a friend in a time of need without having to figure out where to even start.

Because Title IX's goal is to create a sex-based discrimination and harassment-free education, a bunch of its provisions are meant to protect survivors of sexual discrimination or violence from ongoing harassment or trauma. This includes requirements that schools ensure victims do not have to share spaces—like dorms, classes, and campus jobs—with the assailant. And schools are not allowed to make the victim be the person avoiding those shared spaces; they are supposed to remove the assailant.

As you've probably guessed, Title IX also prohibits retaliation against someone reporting sexual discrimination or violence. What you may not know is that not only can a college not retaliate against someone filing a complaint; it must also keep the complaining victim safe from retaliatory harassment or similar behavior from the assailant and the assailant's friends. Schools can, and usually do, issue a no-contact directive, telling the accused that he or she is not permitted from approaching or interacting with the victim. This no-contact directive is usually put in place when the complaint is made, and is meant to protect the victim even before the school's disciplinary procedure is completed.

Schools' procedures for handling sexual discrimination, harassment, and violence differ from how they handle other student-on-student conduct in another important way: schools are prohibited from encouraging, or even allowing, mediation of the complaint. Although with many types of conduct it is beneficial to put students together to "work it out," mediation is not a viable way to resolve sexual discrimination. Asking people to work together to come to resolve their differences when sexual discrimination, harassment, or violence is concerned only serves to re-traumatize the survivor.

One of the most important things to remember about Title IX is that schools *are not allowed* to discourage a survivor from continuing his or her education. This includes suggesting that the student would be better off studying somewhere else. It also means that the college or university should not make the survivor of sexual violence pay for accommodations they require to continue their education after the violence. Tutoring, changes in campus housing, counseling, or other things a sexual violence survivor needs to continue his or her education should be provided by the school at no cost to the student.

If a school violates Title IX, students can file formal Title IX complaints with the Department of Education. Although these complaints can be filed by anyone, I recommend contacting an attorney with experience with the Department of Education to help you through the process.

Other laws dealing with sexual violence at colleges and universities

In Chapter 8 I wrote about the Clery Act and its requirements that schools provide certain information about crime statistics. I also mentioned that the Clery Act would be discussed more in this chapter because of its key role in dealing with sexual violence at school.

The Clery Act contains the Federal Campus Sexual Assault Victims' Bill of Rights.[42] This Bill of Rights requires that schools tell survivors of their options to notify law enforcement, and prohibits schools from discouraging contacting police or encouraging reporting a sexual assault as a lesser offense. It also requires that the accuser and the accused have the same opportunity to have others present during the school's disciplinary procedures, and schools are required to notify both the accuser and the accused of the outcome of any disciplinary proceeding, whatever the outcome. Schools are also required to notify sexual assault survivors about counseling services and options for changing academic and living situations. And these are just some of the highlights. As with Title IX, complaints about schools that fail to comply with the Campus Sexual Assault Victims' Bill of Rights should be made to the U.S. Department of Education. Schools found to have violated this law can be fined up to $35,000 or lose their ability to participate in federal student aid programs.

The Clery Act also partners with Title IX to require that schools provide certain options, information, and resources to survivors of sexual assault, and requires that schools have a prompt and equitable process for resolving complaints.

In 2013, the Violence Against Women Reauthorization Act (VAWA) became law. It did more than just keep the Violence Against Women Act as it was before, it also changed the Clery Act by requiring colleges to "compile statistics for incidents of dating violence, domestic violence, sexual assault, and stalking, and to include certain policies, procedures, and programs pertaining to these incidents in their annual security reports."[43]

Some of the major provisions of the VAWA amendments to the Clery Act, and the resulting regulations, include:

- Colleges are required to keep statistics about the number of dating violence, domestic violence, sexual assault, and stalking incidents;

- Categories of bias for Clery Act hate-crime reporting now include gender identity;

- Colleges are required to give new students and employees their annual security reports;

- Annual Security reports must include:

  o A Statement that the school prohibits dating violence, domestic violence, sexual assault, and stalking;

  o Definitions of dating violence, domestic violence, sexual assault, and stalking;

  o The definition of "consent" in reference to sexual activity;

  o Descriptions of safe and positive options for bystander intervention;

  o Information on risk reduction; and

  o Information on the school's policies and procedures after a sex offense occurs.

- Schools are required to describe each type of disciplinary proceeding the school uses;

- Schools must list the possible punishments for dating violence, domestic violence, sexual assault, or stalking;

- Schools must describe the range of protective measures they offer following an allegation of dating violence, domestic violence, sexual assault, or stalking; and

- Schools must provide a prompt, fair, and impartial disciplinary proceeding that meets with the regulations' requirements.[44]

As with the Campus Sexual Assault Victims' Bill of Rights, schools that don't meet the requirements of Title IX and other parts of the Clery Act can face serious penalties, including fines of up to $35,000 and possibly even the loss of their eligibility to receive federal student aid. As with Title IX violations, if your school fails to comply with the Clery Act, including the amendments, complaints may be filed with the U.S. Department of Education and sometimes in court. Again, although Department of Education complaints can be filed by anyone—and, in theory, anyone can file a court case—I recommend contacting an attorney with experience in this area if you think your school has violated your rights or the rights of others.

Myths surrounding sexual assault and rape

Despite the seriousness of sexual assault and the immense research and study done on it, public perception is far behind reality and several myths persist. At their worst, these myths further harm and traumatize sexual assault survivors and even empower rapists. The importance of debunking these falsehoods cannot be overstated, but unfortunately, a single chapter in a single book is not enough to completely address all the myths that exist.

One persistent myth is that there are "real rapes" and some category of "other" rapes, and that "real rapes" involve a stranger attacking someone. This is blatantly untrue. Most survivors of sexual assault know the person who assaulted them; for both attempted and completed rapes, the survivor knew the offender about 9 times out of 10.[45]

And before moving on, we need to get this out of the way: *Rape is rape*.

There is no "real rape" versus another kind of rape. Whenever someone says something about "real rape" as opposed to what happened to a particular person, they are speaking from an area of ignorance. Although there may be different types of rape, "real rape" and "not real rape" *are not* categories.

Sometimes this "it wasn't really rape" falsehood rears its ugly head when someone wants to blame the survivor for the rape. Rape is *never* the victim's fault. No one ever does or can do anything that entitles another person to sex acts without consent.

Drinking at a party? Too drunk to consent? *Still rape.*

Wearing certain types of clothing? *Still rape.*

Goes to someone's room with them but does not want sex? *Still rape.*

Makes out with someone in their bed but does not want to "go all the way"? *Still rape.*

I've said this once, but I'll say it again: *There's never anything someone can do that makes an unwanted sex act against them anything other than rape.* The only way it's not rape is if there's consent. And the consent must be knowing, ongoing, and not coerced. If at any point someone wants to stop or not go further, consent has been withdrawn.

No one is ever "asking for it." It does not matter if someone took or didn't take any and all available precautions; rape is always—and solely—the fault of the rapist.

I'm not saying that everyone who is accused of rape is a rapist. But neither are false reports common. FBI statistics show that false reporting of sexual assault is in line with that of other major crimes, only 2-8%.[46] In fact, sexual assaults are much more likely to go unreported than they are to be falsely reported.

Some people tend to believe that it's not rape unless the attacker uses force. But because they are often not necessary to force sexual activity on a non-consenting victim, weapons, overt physical force, or even threats are not required for there to be rape. Non-stranger rapists, the great majority of rapists, use the minimal force necessary to overcome resistance; often nothing more than lying on the victim and pinning the arms down, they are far more likely to gain control through deception, manipulation, planning, premeditation, and betraying their victim's trust.[47]

Another myth is that sexual assault victims react hysterically when they are assaulted. But there is no "right way" to react when someone is being sexually assaulted. A sexual assault is a trauma. And one very common response to trauma is the "freeze response." This response is not a choice, but an involuntary psychological response to the trauma. "The freeze response, while a perfectly normal response to trauma, defies the rape myth that a 'real victim' of sexual assault has to resist to the utmost."[48]

There is also no "right way" for someone to act after they have been sexually assaulted. Contrary to common belief, it is not unusual for a sexual assault survivor to continue their relationship with the assailant. Experts conclude that most rape victims maintain a relationship with the assailant and some continue to have sex with the attacker after the assault.[49]

What does it all mean?

I've given you a bunch of information in this chapter. Information on a subject that I sincerely hope none of you has to face on behalf of yourself or anyone you know. But the chances of that are unlikely; based on the statistics, it's very likely that someone you know will be the victim of attempted or completed sexual assault. In a perfect world, the people responsible for sexual assault, mostly men, would simply stop. Since we have yet to discover that perfect world, though, it behooves you to look out for yourself and others.

If you see someone who may be being taken advantage of, step in somehow. If you are planning on engaging in sexual activity with someone, make absolutely sure you have knowing consent (the other person cannot give consent if intoxicated), and always err on the side of assuming you don't have consent. If there is any question as to whether the other person has consented, *then there is no consent.*

I've shown you some things that the government has done and is trying to do to address sexual discrimination, assault, and violence, but the government is not always on your campus, and it won't be at that party or in that dorm room. You might be. You can make a difference. We'll talk in the next chapter about being part of the solution. This will include strategies and ideas about looking out for others and making campuses better, safer places.

SOCIOLOGY
BEING PART OF THE SOLUTION

Bad men need nothing more to compass their ends, than that good men should look on and do nothing.

—*Philosopher John Stuart Mill*[50]

I n the last couple of chapters, I've told you a lot about some very dangerous things that can happen at college. You've seen numbers and statistics, received crazy amounts of information, and hopefully realized that these are serious problems. But they are not problems without solutions. While one person can't end alcohol abuse, hazing, or sexual assault all on their own, each of us can make a difference in our community and at our college, and all of us, working separately and together, can make change happen. We may not be able to eradicate the problems, but at the very least, we can minimize the harms they cause.

The Story of Kitty Genovese

In 1964, The New York Times told the tragic story of Kitty Genovese. Ms. Genovese was returning home around 3:20

AM. As she was walking the 100 feet from her car to her apartment door, she noticed a man at the far end of the parking lot. Thinking something was not right, Ms. Genovese headed up the street where there was a call box to contact police. She didn't make it to the call box. The man grabbed her and stabbed her. She screamed. Lights came on in an apartment building. As Ms. Genovese yelled, "He stabbed me!" A man called down from the apartment, telling the attacker to "Let that girl alone!" The attacker looked up, shrugged, and walked away.[51]

The apartment light went out as Ms. Genovese struggled to her feet and tried to get to her apartment. The attacker came back and stabbed her again. Lights came on and the attacker left her again. But when the lights again went off, he came back. He found Ms. Genovese at the foot of the stairway of her apartment building and stabbed her again, this time killing her.

The attack lasted over 35 minutes and many people saw and heard it. Although not reported in 1964 newspapers, the attack did not just include stabbing, but also rape.[52] In all, 38 people witnessed the rape and murder of Kitty Genovese. No one intervened. No one even called police for more than 35 minutes.

One of the witnesses told police, "I didn't want to get involved."

Assistant Chief Inspector Frederick M. Lussen, who in 1964 had been investigating homicides for 25 years, was shocked. Not because of the murder, but because of all the "good people" who failed to even call police. The New York Times quoted Lussen:

"As we have reconstructed the crime," he said, "the assailant had three chances to kill this woman during a 35-minute period. He returned twice to complete the job. If we had been called when he first attacked, the woman might not be dead now."[53]

Each of the 38 people who saw this crime happen could've done something to stop it. And it wouldn't have required actually confronting the assailant with a knife. A call to the police would likely have saved Kitty Genovese. It may not have even taken that much—if some of the people had left their apartment lights on, it maybe would've been enough to keep the man who killed her away. But people did nothing. They didn't want to get involved, they didn't want to interfere, and they didn't think it was any of their business. So they remained bystanders while something horrible happened.

I'm sure that when they looked back on the event, the witnesses and bystanders wished they had done something, anything, to try to make the situation better. I'm certain many of those 38 people who had an opportunity to do so wished they had simply called the police, or kept their lights on and made sure Ms. Genovese got away from her attacker safely. Doing something other than just standing by and remaining uninvolved may cause certain levels of discomfort when you do it, but it's nothing compared to the discomfort of the regret you might feel knowing you could have done something, but didn't.

If you're thinking an incident that happened more than 50 years ago isn't relevant today, you're wrong. In 2009, outside a high school homecoming dance in California, a 15-year-old was gang-raped. Reports claimed that as many as 20 people watched, cheered, and took pictures on their cell phones while she was robbed, beaten, and gang-raped. These assaults lasted more than two hours until someone who was at the scene talked to someone else at a house party a couple blocks away. The person hearing the report thought something should be done, and eventually, police were called. When the police got there, the assaults were still happening.[54,55]

Even when so many witnesses had cell phones, they used them to take pictures instead of dialing the police to stop this horrendous incident. Unfortunately, Ms. Genovese's case was not a lone occurrence.

What can you do?

Simply standing by is not an option. To paraphrase John Stuart Mill: All that evil needs to flourish is for good people to stand by and do nothing. It's not enough to have the information and be able to notice when something bad is happening. There has to be something you can do. And there are things you can do, things that don't require that you place yourself in danger or put yourself in a horribly uncomfortable situation. No matter what the problem is that you see, there is something that you can do to stop it and protect potential victims.

It's so important to *do something*.

When you are there, seeing a situation occur, and you are not directly part of it, you are a bystander. But when you are a bystander, you don't have to remain one, and it's not a reason to let something happen when you can protect someone.

Bystander intervention does not always, or even usually, require direct confrontation. You can usually accomplish the goal of your intervention without putting yourself into an overly vulnerable state. What you do need, though, is the ability and strength to trust yourself. If you think a situation needs some intervention, then you should intervene. Be confident enough in yourself, your moral compass, and your danger-detection abilities to take some action.

Remember, you're part of the community, and whatever happens will affect you and others in the community.

Why do bystanders stand by?

There have been a bunch of studies done over many years to try to figure out why people don't respond and intervene. The biggest three reasons that have been found are audience inhibition, social influence, and diffusion of responsibility.[56] Audience inhibition is the fear by bystanders that others might view their response negatively if they take action, especially if it turns out that what they thought was an emergency situation wasn't. The more people present, the greater the risk, and the less likely the bystander is to intervene. Social influence deals with the fact that most apparent helping situations are ambiguous—you can't tell whether it's really an emergency or not. The presence of other people contributes to a bystander not acting, because the bystander looks to other people to help define whether the situation is an emergency. When bystanders are all looking at each other for clues as to what the appropriate response is, they each see the inaction of the others and interpret the situation as not-so-critical or decide that the socially accepted behavior is not to intervene. Lastly, diffusion of responsibility is a conscious or subconscious way to reduce the psychological cost—or "guilt factor"—of not intervening. If there are a bunch of other people around, and none of them intervene either, then the bystander shifts some of the responsibility on to them to help; this essentially allows the bystander not to feel too guilty if they don't help, because there were other people who also take a share of the blame.[57]

Another common reason bystanders may not intervene is the fear of retaliation. Sometimes, bystanders are scared that if they intervene, especially confrontationally, they will face negative consequences physically, emotionally, or psychologically.

And lastly, another reason why bystanders do not intervene is that, despite being conflicted and confused themselves, they see others' inaction and come to think it's because everyone else believes that no one should act. "Despite knowing that their calm public façade belies their conflicted, uncertain, and confused internal state, they assume that the public presentations of others correspond to equally calm interiors, thereby implying that there is no cause for alarm."[58] In other words: you're not acting because you don't know what to do, but you assume everyone else is not acting because they know not to.

Pluralistic ignorance not only causes bystanders to fail to intervene in situations where they should, but it can also cause behaviors and ideas to continue as social norms even though they are not supported by most people—most people don't like it, but everyone assumes it's okay with everybody but them, so the situation continues.

Researchers have identified four stages in the process of moving bystanders from inaction to action. These stages are normally gone through one at a time as people go from seeing a problem to doing something about it. The four stages are:

1. Notice the event;
2. See it as a problem;
3. Feel responsible for dealing with it; and
4. Possess the necessary skills to act.[59]

Only after moving through all of these stages will a bystander act.

Notice the event and see it as a problem

A large portion of chapters 9, 10, and 11 were dedicated to helping you notice events and see problems as problems. Some of the biggest problems you are likely to see at college may involve alcohol use, hazing, and sexual violence. But there are other situations where bystander intervention would be helpful toward making communities better places. Situations where people use terms and phrases that are offensive to certain groups, or just offensive in general—things like, "That's so gay," or using the word "rape" to talk about anything other than actual rape, or using ethnic, religious, or other slurs. Bystander intervention can even be used when people express approval over dangerous behavior, like getting really drunk at a party, driving intoxicated, or talking like something illegal or stupidly dangerous was really cool.

These are all situations where bystander intervention can make a difference. Some situations are easy to notice and see as problems, like seeing the precursors to a sexual assault, or seeing someone being beat up. Others may not be so obvious. When it comes to people saying things like, "That's so gay," or "So-and-so totally raped me in that game last night," it's easy for some to brush it off as, "that's just how that person talks. Sure, it's offensive, but he doesn't mean anything by it." That doesn't make it right or even okay. If the behavior makes you uncomfortable, trust yourself and note it as a problem.

Feel responsible for dealing with it

This is where the train often leaves the track when it comes to bystander intervention. If you're even a little bit worried or nervous about stepping in, it can be really easy to say it's not your responsibility and stay out of it. One way of passing off responsibility is thinking that you're not socially significant enough to make a difference, or that someone older, or more established, or more respected should take care of the problem. Other people don't feel responsibility because they don't think they are part of the problem; if they don't use homophobic language themselves, then it's not their responsibility to make sure others don't either.

One way to get over your inclination not to take responsibility is realizing that mistreatment does not just hurt the people mistreated, it hurts others too. If you want to be part of the solution, you have to do something about the problem even if you didn't cause it. Remember the quote from the beginning of this chapter? "All that evil needs to prosper is for good people to do nothing." There are bumper stickers and other things that display the quote, "Be the change you want to see in the world." Although Gandhi probably never actually said this, even though it's repeatedly attributed to him, there is something to it. If you want to see the world change, change it. And Eldridge Cleaver did say, "If you are not part of the solution, you are a part of the problem."

If you know something is wrong, take responsibility to help change it.

Possess the necessary skills to act

This is really where it comes all together, isn't it. It doesn't do much good to notice a situation, see it as a problem, and accept responsibility for doing something about it if you don't know how to address it effectively. So what can you do? How can you effectively intervene?

Often, when people think of bystander intervention, they think of direct intervention, and specifically, confrontation.

While direct confrontation of someone who is causing a problem is one possible solution, it's not always the best. And to many people, it is not the palatable response. But direct intervention can also involve approaching the person who is on the receiving end of the wrongful behavior, or just offering to help someone without necessarily explicitly opposing their behavior. An example of helping someone without directly opposing behavior would be to offer to call a cab for someone who has been drinking, or offer to walk them home so they don't have to walk alone.

Sometimes, direct intervention doesn't even need to happen right while the behavior is taking place. Certainly, if the behavior that needs to be stopped is an assault in progress, you need to act immediately. But if it's a crude joke someone makes, or someone is getting drunk more than they should but is not in any immediate danger, sometimes it is better to intervene later. It doesn't do much good to talk to someone who is really wasted about why they shouldn't get so drunk so often; and if someone is making racist or sexist jokes to a group of people, depending on the situation, it may be better to talk to them about it in private.

Not all intervention has to be direct. Indirect intervention can be anything done to intervene in the situation that does not involve inserting yourself into the situation. In certain, severe cases, the most effective and necessary type of indirect intervention is to call the police or other authorities. If you think the situation needs a police presence, you should call. Don't assume someone else is going to do it, and don't assume that the situation does not call for action just because no one else is acting on it.

Another kind of indirect intervention involves speaking with other bystanders. This indirect intervention can be with other people who see the problematic behavior and are offended by or concerned with it. Sometimes indirect intervention like this can help you overcome pluralistic ignorance, giving you real information that other people are also concerned, and help you directly intervene if necessary.

Aside from direct and indirect intervention, bystanders can often defuse problematic behavior, or the effects of problematic behavior, through distraction. Not everyone looks at this as separate from direct or indirect intervention—likely because you can distract in a direct or indirect way—but there are enough differences that you should at least look at it as an option of its own. One benefit of viewing distraction as something other than direct intervention is that it removes any lingering apprehension about confronting someone engaged in problem behavior.

Distraction is a useful intervention technique in many circumstances. If someone is telling racist or sexist jokes or harassing people, you could ask them for the time or for directions to break them out of their pattern; or if it's a conversation you are part of, you may be able to simply change the subject. Distraction can also allow a potential target of dangerous behavior to get away, or give others a chance to intervene directly with the potential assailant or potential victim. If you see a situation that looks like harassment or potential sexual violence, you can distract the potential offender by interrupting and starting a conversation. And if you've spoken with others who agree that the situation is potentially dangerous, they can help the potential victim out of harm's way while the potential offender is engaged with you.

Being part of the solution

It's not always easy to be part of the solution. A lot of times it seems much simpler to just stay out of the way. But if you see a problem, you need to be part of the solution. It would be hard to look back on college and consider yourself successful when you can't get past that time you saw a person in danger, knew he or she needed help, and did nothing.

You've got the tools now to notice and respond to some of the biggest potential problems at school, or anywhere in life. When that little voice inside you starts telling you something is wrong, you can bet you're not the only one feeling that way. And just because you may not see others acting on that feeling, doesn't mean they don't feel the same way or that you shouldn't act.

Help make college successful for you *and* everyone else.

Be part of the solution.

COMMENCEMENT

YOU GOT THIS

"Commencement" is a great word. It's what a graduation ceremony is called, but it also means "the beginning." Your high school commencement was the end to one era of your life and the beginning of college. And your college commencement is even bigger, as both an end and a beginning.

Since we're at the end of this book, I want to focus on a couple types of commencement. Let's start with beginning your college experience. I almost typed "college career" there, but that makes it sound like a job, or like I'm buying into the whole "college as career training" view, which I don't. College is many things. Above all, it is an experience and an opportunity. It is a time to grow into you.

You'll face challenges in college. And I sincerely hope this book will help you through many of them, and help you avoid the challenges that you don't need to face. Define what college success means for you, and achieve it. You've got the tools, now you just need to use them.

As you get ready to start college, or if you're reading this after you've already started, as you ready yourself for the next part of your college experience, remember that success is up to you. And remember: success is not reserved for certain people with certain gifts; it is available to everyone. It may not be possible for everyone to leave college with a perfect 4.0 GPA—I know I didn't—but a 4.0 is not necessary for success. It isn't even always an indicator of success. College success is becoming a better you, and getting closer to the person you are supposed to be.

Yes, grades are an important part of college success. You need to do the best you possibly can academically because, ultimately, you go to "institutions of higher education" to get an education. But success is also about so much more.

Success can be achieved by anyone with the right tools and the willingness to use those tools to their fullest. You've started putting together the tools. And if you need more, they're available—some through U Ready, some elsewhere. But now you know where to start looking.

So commence your college experience with the knowledge that you have what it takes to succeed. You know how to achieve academic success, and you have the tools to go through college safely and to make it a better place for you and those around you. You know the dangers and some of the important issues, and you have the facts to face them and speak about them from an informed standpoint.

Finishing college and starting strong

If you've used the tools you have and had a successful college experience, you'll eventually graduate. You'll go through another commencement that marks the end of your college experience and the start of the rest of your life. I don't want to call this "entering the real world," because college is certainly real. There will be more big changes and challenges as you leave college and begin your next step, whether it is grad school, a career, or any other option. But the tools you've used to reach college success will help you in the next step, too.

Remember Seneca's quote from the beginning of this book? "Luck is what happens when preparation meets opportunity." The tools in this book helped you prepare for college; your college experience helps prepare you for the next step in life. But these aren't sequential, they're incremental. The tools that helped you through college will also help in the next experience, and the tools are far from useless once you finish college.

Be prepared. Be confident. You've got what it takes to succeed in college. Let me be the first to congratulate you on your success.

And let me also be the first to encourage you on the next experience.

You've got the tools.

You've proven you have the ability and drive to succeed.

A successful life is full of continued learning and growing. Never be content to just stay where you are. Keep pushing boundaries. Don't close your mind. Be open to new possibilities. I'm significantly older than you, and I'm still learning new things about the world. Maybe even more importantly, I'm still learning new things about myself.

Use every experience to grow. And always, *always* remember: success is not an unattainable goal; it's there for you to grab it.

You got this.

ENDNOTES

1 Jaison Abel and Richard Deitz, "Agglomeration and Job Matching among College Graduates," *Staff Report No. 587* (2014). Although this study only takes undergraduate degrees into account, it shows that a large number of people do not end up in a career related to their college major.

2 *Monty Python and the Holy Grail*, directed by Terry Gilliam & Terry Jones (1975; United Kingdom: EMI Films).

3 Annie Dillard, *The Writing Life*, (New York: HarperCollins Publishers, 1990).

4 Bryan A. Garner, *Garner's Modern American Usage*, 3rd ed. (Oxford: Oxford University Press, 2009) 587.

5 Garner, *Garner's Modern American Usage.*

6 Ibid.

7 Dave Barry, *Dave Barry's Bad Habits* (New York: Henry Holt and Company, LLC.: 1985) 200.

8 If you're planning top major in philosophy, or something like contemporary English literature, please don't be too upset that I separated such things from what I described as "practical" majors. Know that I wouldn't go back and major in something other than philosophy if I had the chance.

9 H.W. Turnbull, ed., *The Correspondence of Isaac Newton: 1661-1675* (London: Published for the Royal Society at University Press, 1959), 416.
Even in this quote, Newton was "standing on the shoulders" of giants. The idea in this quote can be dated back at least as far as 1159, to The Metalogican of John of Salisbury.

10 The Jeanne Clery Disclosure of Campus Security Policy and Campus Crime Statistics Act, 20 U.S.C. § 1092(f); implementing regulations at 34 C.F.R. 668.46.

11 For more information on the Clery Act, visit the Clery Center for Security on Campus at clerycenter.org.

12 Substance Abuse and Mental Health Services Administration, *Results from the 2014 National Survey on Drug Use and Health: Table 6.88B—Alcohol use in the past month among persons aged 18 to 22, by college enrollment status and demographic characteristics: Percentages, 2013 and 2014*, Accessed: http://www.samhsa.gov/data/sites/default/files/NSDUH-DetTabs2014/NSDUH-DetTabs2014.htm#tab6-88b

13 Substance Abuse and Mental Health Services Administration, *Results from the 2014 National Survey on Drug Use and Health: Table 6.89B—Binge alcohol use in the past month among persons aged 18 to 22, by college enrollment status and demographic characteristics: Percentages, 2013 and 2014*, Accessed: http://www.samhsa.gov/data/sites/default/files/NSDUH-DetTabs2014/NSDUH-DetTabs2014.htm#tab6-89b; Substance Abuse and Mental Health Services Administration, *Results from the 2014 National Survey on Drug Use and Health: Table 6.90B—Heavy alcohol use in the past month among persons aged 18 to 22, by college enrollment status and demographic characteristics: Percentages, 2013 and 2014*, Accessed: http://www.samhsa.gov/data/sites/default/files/NSDUH-DetTabs2014/NSDUH-DetTabs2014.htm#tab6-90b.

14 R.W. Hingson, W. Zha, an E.R. Weitzman, "Magnitude of and trends in alcohol-related mortality and morbidity among U.S. college students ages 18–24, 1998–2005," *Journal of Studies on Alcohol and Drugs* 16 (2009): 12–20.

15 R.W. Hingson et al., "Magnitude of alcohol-related mortality and morbidity among U.S. college students ages 18–24: Changes from 1998 to 2001," *Annual Review of Public Health* 26 (2005): 259–279.

16 Ibid.

17 *Alcohol Facts and Statistics.* National Institute on Alcohol Abuse and Alcoholism. C. Blanco et al., "Mental health of college students and their non-college-attending peers: Results from the National Epidemiologic Study on Alcohol and Related Conditions," *Archives of General Psychiatry* 65 (2008): 1429–1437.

18 H. Wechsler et al., "Changes in binge drinking and related problems among American college students between 1993 and 1997: Results of the Harvard School of Public Health College Alcohol Study," *Journal of American College Health* 47 (1998): 57–68.

19 *"Drunk or dying?* you make the call," is a phrase coined by, and used courtesy of, Aware Awake Alive, awareawakealive.org.

20 "MUST HELP" and recommended actions used with permission of Aware Awake Alive, and can be found online at http://awareawakealive.org/educate/know-the-signs.

21 Hank, Nuwer, "Hazing Deaths," accessed April 15, 2016, www.hanknuwer.com/articles/hazing-deaths/.

22 See *In the Matter of Khalil H.*, 910 N.Y.S.2d 553, 80 A.D.3d 83 (2010).

23 Elizabeth Allan and Mary Madden, *Hazing in View: College Students at Risk, Initial Findings from the National Study of Student Hazing,* 2008, accessed: www.stophazing.org/hazing-view.

24 While 2008 may seem like a long time ago, hazing has been occurring—dangerous and deadly—for such a long time that the findings are still more-than-worth looking at.

25 Allen and Madden. *Hazing in View: College Students at Risk, Initial Findings from the National Study of Student Hazing.* www.stophazing.org/hazing-view.

26 Ibid., 36.

27 Dave Westol, "The Three Deadly Nights," *The FRMT Risk Management Newsletter* 16 (2005): 1.

28 Allen and Madden. *Hazing in View: College Students at Risk, Initial Findings from the National Study of Student Hazing,* 2.

29 Senate Select Committee on Intelligence, *The Official Senate Report On CIA Torture: Committee Study of the Central*

Intelligence Agency's Detention and Interrogation Program, prepared by Dianne Feinstein and John McCain, (Washington, D.C.: U.S. United States Government Printing Office, 2014), 113-288.
30   Westol, "The Three Deadly Nights," 1.
31   *McKenzie v. State of Maryland*, 131 Md.App. 124, 148 n12, 748 A.2d 67 (2000).
32   Allen and Madden. *Hazing in View: College Students at Risk, Initial Findings from the National Study of Student Hazing*, 25.
33   Allen and Madden. *Hazing in View: College Students at Risk, Initial Findings from the National Study of Student Hazing*, 33.
34   Allen and Madden. *Hazing in View: College Students at Risk, Initial Findings from the National Study of Student Hazing*, 33-34.
35   Nancy Chi Cantalupo, "Burying Our Heads in the Sand: lack of Knowledge, Knowledge Avoidance, and the Persistent Problem of Campus Peer Sexual Violence," *Loyola University Chicago Law Journal* 43 (2011): p. 205, 209-210; Brenda J. Benson et al., "College Women and Sexual Assault: The Role of Sex-Related Alcohol Expectancies," *Journal of Family Violence* 22 (2007): 341, 348; see also Carol Bohmer and Andrea Parrot, *Sexual Assault on Campus: The Problem and the Solution* (New York: Lexington Books, 1993); United States Department of Justice, *The Sexual Victimization of College Women,* reported prepared by Bonnie s. Fisher et al, 2000, Accessed: http://ncjrs.gov/pdffiles1/nij/182369.pdf.
36   United States Department of Justice, *Rape and sexual assault: Reporting to police and medical attention, 192-2000,* report prepared by C.A. Rennison, 2002, Accessed: http://bjs.ojp.usdoj.gov/content/pub/pdf/rsarp00.pdf.
37   United States Department of Justice, *The Sexual Victimization of College Women,* reported prepared by Bonnie s. Fisher et al, 2000, Accessed: http://ncjrs.gov/pdffiles1/nij/182369.pdf.
38   Nancy Cantalupo, "Burying Our Heads in the Sand: lack of Knowledge, Knowledge Avoidance, and the Persistent Problem of Campus Peer Sexual Violence." *Loyola University*

Chicago Law Journal 43 (2011); citing United States Department of Justice, *The Campus Sexual Assault Study: Final Report 5-3* report prepared by Krebs et al., 2007, Accessed: http://www.ncjrs.gov/pdffiles1/nij/grants221153.pdf; Carol Bohmer and Andrea Parrot, *Sexual Assault on Campus: The Problem and the Solution* (New York: Lexington Books, 1993).

[39] United States Department of Justice, *The Sexual Victimization of College Women,* reported prepared by Bonnie s. Fisher et al, 2000, Accessed: http://ncjrs.gov/pdffiles1/nij/182369. pdf.

[40] Title IX, Education Amendments of 1972, 20 U.S.C. §1981(a).

[41] "Know Your IX," http://knowyourix.org/title-ix/ title-ix-the-basics/.

[42] Jeanne Clery Act, 20 U.S.C. §1092(g).

[43] Department of Education, *Federal Register* 79 (2014): accessed: https://www.gpo.gov/fdsys/pkg/FR-2014-10-20/ pdf/2014-24284.pdf.

[44] Ibid.

[45] United States Department of Justice, *The Sexual Victimization of College Women,* reported prepared by Bonnie s. Fisher et al, 2000, Accessed: http://ncjrs.gov/pdffiles1/nij/182369. pdf.

[46] Susan Brownmiller, *Against Our Will: Men, Women and Rape* (New York: Ballentine Books, 1993).

[47] Teresa P. Scalzo, Esq., "Overcoming the Consent Defense," *Violence Against Women Newsletter* 5 (2007) accessed: http:// www.mncasa.org/assets/PDFs/APRI%20Consent%20 Defense.pdf.

[48] Wisconsin Office of Justice Assistance, *Wisconsin Prosecutor's Sexual Assault Reference Book*, 2009, accessed: https:// www.wcasa.org/file_open.php?id=3.

[49] Patricia L. Fanflik, "Victim Responses to Sexual Assault: Counterintuitive or Simply Adaptive?" *Office of Violence Against Women Special Topics Series* (2007) accessed: https://archive. org/details/604804-report-victim-responses-to-sexual-assault.

50 John Stuart Mill, *Inaugural Address Delivered to the University of St. Andrews Feb. 1st 1867* (London: Longmans, Green, Reader, and Dyer, 1867), 36.

51 Except as otherwise noted, the details surrounding the attack and murder of Kitty Genovese are taken from: Martin Gansberg, "37 Who Saw Murder Didn't Call the Police," *New York Times,* March 27, 1964, accessed: http://www.nytimes.com/1964/03/27/37-who-saw-murder-didnt-call-the-police.html?_r=0.

52 Robert D. McFadden, "Winston Mosely, Who Killed Kitty Genovese, Dies in Prison at 81," *New York Times,* April 4, 2016, accessed: http://www.nytimes.com/2016/04/05/nyregion/winston-moseley-81-killer-of-kitty-genovese-dies-in-prison.html.

53 Gansberg, "37 Who Saw Murder Didn't Call the Police," *New York Times.*

54 Karl Fisher and Shelly Meron, "Police Arrest Second Teen in Connection with Gang Rape on 15-Year-Old Girl," *Costa Rica Times,* October 26, 2009, accessed: http://www.mercurynews.com/ci_13644237.

55 "Police: People Watched Gang Rape of Teen and did Nothing to Help," *Huffington Post,* March 18, 2010, accessed: http://www.huffingtonpost.com/2009/10/27/police-people-watched-gan_n_334975.html.

56 Bibb Latané and Steve Nida, "Ten Years of Research on Group Size and Helping," *Psychological Bulletin,* 89 (1981): 308-324, accessed https://www.uni-muenster.de/imperia/md/content/psyifp/aeechterhoff/sommersemester2012/schluesselstudiendersozialpsychologiea/latanenida_bystandereffgroupsize_psybull1981.pdf.

57 Gansberg, "37 Who Saw Murder Didn't Call the Police," *New York Times.*
Latané and Nida, "Ten Years of Research on Group Size and Helping," 308-324.

58 Dale T. Miller and Leif D. Nelson, "Seeing Approach Motivation in the Avoidance Behavior of Others: Implications for an Understanding of Pluralistic Ignorance," *Journal of*

Personality and Social Psychology 83 (2002) accessed: http://givingandappreciating.com/wp-content/uploads/2013/03/Seeing-Approach-Motivation-in-the-Avoidance-Behavior-of-Others_-Implications-for-an-Understanding-of-Pluralistic-Ignorance.pdf.

[59] Alan Berkowitz, *Response Ability: A Complete Guide to Bystander Intervention*, (Chicago: Beck & Company, 2009) 9-10.

SPECIAL THANKS

A whole bunch of things had to happen for this book to come together. I'm sure I could fill another book the length of this one if I thanked each and every person who helped along the way. I sincerely apologize to anyone who is left out.

Huge thanks to my wife, Tara, and the kids, Xander, Xavier, Malcolm, Quilan, and Amara. You all are my inspiration and my biggest supporters. Thank you for being there for me when I needed you, and for your encouragement as I brought the book to publication.

Thank you to all of the college students who have had to deal with me in one way or another through the years; the successes I've seen from so many of you made me want to write this book to make sure everyone had an opportunity to meet your achievements.

To my extended family and friends—Mom and Dad, Mom N., Tony and Shannon, Candi and Zack, Scott (Scooter, Sved...), Shannon (different Shannon), Chris, Frig, Stephen, and so many more—I can't express the different ways you're all part of this book and the writing of it.

Professionally, thank you to Aware Awake Alive for MUST HELP and for all the work you do to make the world a better place. Thank you Alan Berkowitz for your work in bystander intervention. Thank you Doug for introducing me to many of the topics in this book and showing me how serious they are. And Gary, thank you for giving the first spark to my collegiate teaching career.

Kary, thanks for the coaching and the introduction to so many great people and authors. As always, you showed up filled up. Thank you for letting me is part of your program.

I'd like to thank God for all of the experiences that led me to this place and allowed me to write this book.

And lastly, readers, I'd like to thank you for trusting me to help you through one of the biggest transitions in your life. Please let me know how *The U Solution* has helped you, or what you've learned. You can always contact me at *UReady.net*

ABOUT THE AUTHOR

Joshua D. Sheffer graduated *cum laude* from Notre Dame Law School and practiced general civil litigation for almost 15 years before accepting his first appointment in full-time academia. He was bitten by the teaching bug when began as an adjunct professor teaching legal studies courses at a local college while he practiced law full time. He is now an assistant professor at a State university.

Before teaching, Joshua was part of a nationwide practice representing the victims and survivors of school violence. While part of that practice, he became aware of the extreme need for total college preparation, and not just the academic preparation so many guides focus on. This led

Joshua to write *The U Solution* and start U Ready, LLC, a company dedicated to making sure students are fully prepared for college.

When not "professoring" for the university or writing, speaking, and otherwise working through U Ready to help students, Joshua enjoys spending time with his wife Tara and their five children. He lives in northwest Michigan and can be reached at *UReady.net*

U Ready?

Parent/Student Guide

Preparing for college is never easy, and it's even harder to do it alone. It doesn't help that many parents and first-time college students don't know what to expect and what to talk about. Parents and students can work together using U Ready's Parent/Student Guide, which will take you through *The U Solution* chapter-by-chapter with helpful and practical exercises, tips, discussion topics, and more.

Available Winter 2016

 More at *UReady.net*

BRING JOSHUA TO YOUR GROUP

AUTHOR. SPEAKER. TEACHER. LAWYER.

It is important that you choose the right speaker for your group. The right one will inspire your group and set them on the right path for success; the wrong one will bore them. Joshua's direct and authentic approach combine with his content to make him a top choice for groups of students, parents, or both. Each message or workshop is customized to achieve and exceed your group's goals.

CONTACT JOSHUA TODAY TO BEGIN THE CONVERSATION
UReady.net

U Ready?

We'll Help You Get There

It's impossible to completely cover every aspect of the topics included in *The U Solution* in a single book. Dive deeper and get even more helpful information, tools, and strategies to help define and achieve total college success.

Find Out More at UReady.net

You Got This!